Narcissistic Abuse Recovery

The Ultimate Guide to Heal Your Psychology Wounds. Discover Effective Strategies to Stop Toxic Relationships and Overcome Anxiety. Start Loving Yourself Again.

Jennet Brown

© Copyright 2021 by Jennet Brown - All rights reserved.

ISBN: 978-1-80271-007-6

This document is geared towards providing exact and reliable information in regards to the topic and issue covered. The publication is sold with the idea that the publisher is not required to render accounting, officially permitted, or otherwise, qualified services. If advice is necessary, legal or professional, a practiced individual in the profession should be ordered.

- From a Declaration of Principles, which was accepted and approved equally by a Committee of the American Bar Association and a Committee of Publishers and Associations.

In no way is it legal to reproduce, duplicate, or transmit any part of this document in either electronic means or printed format. Recording of this publication is strictly prohibited, and any storage of this document is not allowed unless with written permission from the publisher. All rights reserved.

The information provided herein is stated to be truthful and consistent. In terms of inattention or otherwise, any liability, by any usage or abuse of any policies, processes, or directions contained within is the solitary and utter responsibility of the recipient reader. Under no circumstances will any legal responsibility or blame be held against the publisher for reparation, damages, or monetary loss due to the information herein, either directly or indirectly.

Respective authors own all copyrights not held by the publisher.

The information herein is offered for informational purposes solely and is universal as such. The presentation of the information is without a contract or any type of guarantee assurance.

The trademarks used are without any consent, and the publication of the trademark is without permission or backing by the trademark owner. All trademarks and brands within this book are for clarifying purposes only and are owned by the owners themselves, not affiliated with this document.

Table of Contents

INTRODUCTION   9

CHAPTER 1 WHAT'S NARCISSISTIC PERSONALITY DISORDER (NPD)?   12

SIGNS AND SYMPTOMS OF NARCISSISTIC PERSONALITY DISORDER   14
GRANDIOSE SENSE OF SELF-IMPORTANCE   14
LIVES IN A DREAM WORLD THAT AFFIRMS THEIR DELUSIONS OF GRANDEUR   15
REQUIRES CONSTANT COMPLIMENTS AND RESPECT   15
SENSE OF ENTITLEMENT   16
EXPLOITS OTHERS WITHOUT REMORSE OR SHAME   16
OFTEN DEMEANS, INTIMIDATES, BULLIES, OR BELITTLES OTHER PEOPLE   17
DO NOT FALL FOR THE DREAM   17
SET HEALTHY BOUNDARIES   19
DO NOT TAKE THINGS PERSONALLY   21
START LOOKING FOR PURPOSE AND SUPPORT ELSEWHERE   22
THE WAY TO MAKE A NARCISSIST   24
WHEN YOU'VE LEFT   25
IF YOU WANT AID FOR NARCISSISTIC PERSONALITY DISORDER   27
IDENTIFYING NARCISSISTIC PERSONALITY DISORDER TRAITS   28
INDICATORS OF NARCISSISTIC PERSONALITY DISORDER   29
REASONS FOR NARCISSISTIC PERSONALITY DISORDER   31
REMEDY FOR NARCISSISTIC PERSONALITY DISORDER   32
WHAT IS THE PROGNOSIS FOR SOMEBODY WITH REA A PERSONALITY DISORDER?   34
LIVING TOGETHER WITH NARCISSISTIC PERSONALITY DISORDER   34
WHAT ARE THE NINE TRAITS OF A NARCISSIST?   34
NINE SIGNS AND SYMPTOMS OF NARCISSISM   35
1. GRANDIOSITY   35
2. EXCESSIVE DEMAND FOR RESPECT   35
3. SUPERFICIAL AND EXPLOITATIVE RELATIONSHIPS   35
4. DEFICIENCY OF COMPASSION   36
5. IDENTITY DISTURBANCE   36
7. PERSISTENT FEELINGS OF EMPTINESS AND BOREDOM   36
8. VULNERABILITY TO LIFE ALTERATIONS   37

WHAT'S NARCISSISM DIAGNOSED?	37
WHAT IS THE TREATMENT FOR NARCISSISM?	38
TYPES	41
VINTAGE	41
VULNERABLE	42
COMMUNAL	43
MALIGNANT	43
SUB-TYPE 1: OVERT VS. COVERT	44
SUB-TYPE 2: SOMATIC VS. CEREBRAL	45
SUB-TYPE 3: INVERTED VS. SADISTIC	46
REASONS	46
WARNING SIGNS	49
DIFFERENT TYPES OF NARCISSISTS & THE WAY TO MOTIVATE THEM	52
JUST HOW VARIOUS KINDS OF NARCISSISM ARE YOU?	52
1. HEALTHFUL NARCISSISM	53
2. GRANDIOSE NARCISSISM	54
5. PHYSICAL NARCISSISM	55
6. SOMATIC NARCISSISM	56
7. CEREBRAL NARCISSIST	57
8. SPIRITUAL NARCISSIST	57

CHAPTER 2 NARCISSISTIC ABUSE CHIEF FACETS?   59

1. NAME-CALLING	61
2. CONDESCENSION	62
3. CRITICISM	62
4. DEGRADATION	62
6. BLAME	63
7. ACCUSATIONS	64
8. WITHHOLDING OR ISOLATION	64
10. CIRCULAR ARGUMENTS	65
11. HAZARDS	66
WHAT TO DO	66
THE WAY TO SPOT AND RESPOND TO EMOTIONAL BLACKMAIL	67
WHAT IS THE DEFINITION?	67
HOW IT WORKS	67
1. DEMAND	68
2. RESISTANCE	68

3. Stress	68
4. Hazards	69
5. Compliance	70
6. Repetition	70
Frequent examples	71
Punishers	71
Self-punishers	72
Sufferers	72
The Way to respond to this	74
First, recognize what is not emotional blackmail	74
Keep calm and stall	75
Begin a conversation	75
Identify your triggers	76
Enlist them compromise	77
Typical Traits of Narcissists and Gaslighters	77
1. Frequent Lies and Exaggerations	78
2. Rarely Admit Flaws and Why Are Aggressive When Criticized	78
3. False Image Projection	79
4. Rule Breaking and Boundary Violation	80
5. Emotional Invalidation and Coercion	81
6. Manipulation	82
Hoovering and the Narcissistic Victim	84
How can this occur? Why would somebody knowingly return to a violent relationship?	85
Step One	85
Step Two	86
Step Three	86
Reasons a narcissist participates in hovering:	88
What do you have to cure and put yourself free?	96
The Way to handle the lure	99
The Way to Establish Boundaries With A Narcissist	101
Insidious Ways Narcissistic Abuse Isolates that the Victim	105
How Narcissistic Abuse Isolates	106
1. Narcissistic Abuse Isolates You against the External World	106
2. Narcissistic Abuse Isolates You from Family Members	107
3. Narcissistic Abuse Isolates You Yourself	107
4. Narcissistic Abuse Isn't Understood	108

CHAPTER 3 TRAITS NARCISSISTS SEARCH FOR THEIR VICTIMS 110

TRAIT NUMBER ONE: UNHEALED TRAUMAS 110
TRAIT NUMBER 2: NOT HONOURING YOUR INNER BEING 111
TRAIT NUMBER THREE: NOT GETTING YOUR OWN WHOLE LIFE 113
TRAIT NUMBER FIVE: ATTEMPTING TO CHANGE OTHERS TO STOP THEM FROM HURTING YOU 116
TRAIT NUMBER SIX: YOU AREN'T SELF-PARTNERED AND LOVING YOURSELF 118
THE WAY TO RECUPERATE FROM ALL THESE SIX TRAITS 119
1. CONSCIENTIOUSNESS. 121
2. EMPATHY. 122
3. INTEGRITY. 123
4. RESILIENCE. 124
5. A HIGH AMOUNT OF SENTIMENTALITY. 125

CHAPTER 4 COPING WITH A NARCISSISTIC PERSONALITY 128

1. WATCH THEM FOR WHO THEY'RE 128
2. BREAK THE CHARM AND STOP FOCUSING ON THEM 129
3. SPEAK UP FOR YOURSELF 130
4. ESTABLISH CLEAR BOUNDARIES 131
FOR EXAMPLE 132
5. EXPECT THEM TO DRIVE BACK 132
6. BEAR IN MIND THAT YOU'RE NOT AT FAULT 132
7. LOCATE A SERVICE SYSTEM 133
WHAT'S A HEALTHY RELATIONSHIP? 134
8. INSIST ON IMMEDIATE ACTIONS, NOT PROMISES 134
9. UNDERSTAND A REAL PERSON MAY WANT PROFESSIONAL ASSISTANCE 135
10. RECOGNIZE WHEN YOU NEED ASSISTANCE 135
WHEN TO PROCEED 136
THE WAY TO HANDLE NARCISSISTIC ABUSE 137
THE MOTIVATION FOR NARCISSISTIC ABUSE 138
MISTAKES IN MANAGING ABUSE 139
1. CONFRONT ABUSE EFFICIENTLY. 141
2. KNOW YOUR RIGHTS. 141
3. BE ASSERTIVE. 142

4. BE STRATEGIC. 142
5. SET BOUNDARIES. 142
6. HAVE CONSEQUENCES. 143
7. BE EDUCATIVE. 143
CHAPTER 5 THE WAY TO CURE FROM NARCISSISTIC ABUSE **144**
CORE INSIGHTS FROM A NARCISSISTIC ABUSE RECOVERY COACH 144
HOW CAN I HEAL FROM NARCISSISTIC ABUSE? 148
WHAT EXACTLY DOES NARCISSISTIC ABUSE DO FOR YOU? 148
THE IMPACTS OF NARCISSISTIC ABUSE 148
WHAT HAPPENS AFTER YOU STAND UP TO YOUR NARCISSIST? 150
HOW CAN YOU FEEL AFTER HAVING A NARCISSIST? 150
HOW DO YOU RECOVER FROM NARCISSISTIC ABUSE? 151
CONCLUSION 153

Introduction

A narcissist is a frequent catchphrase describing somebody who behaves self-absorbed or vainly. A lot of don't understand that narcissism, or narcissistic personality disorder (NPD), is really a significant illness. When you've got NPD identification, others might see you as just concerned about your needs and wants or using a never-ending demand for compliments. But indoors, you might feel insecure, less-than and vacant. Having NPD makes it difficult to relate to other people or have real self-worth. It may impact relationships with your loved ones, friends and co-workers. Experts estimate that around 5 percent of individuals have NPD. Narcissism is just one of 10 character disorders. These illnesses cause people to believe, feel and act in a way that harms others or themselves. Signals of personality disorders usually arise in the late teen years and early maturity.

Healthcare providers diagnose NPD if you've five of the following attributes:
- Over inflated sense of self-importance.
- Constant ideas about being more powerful, strong, smart, adored or appealing than others.

- Feelings of excellence and want to just associate with high-status men and women.
- Requirement for excess admiration.
- Sense of entitlement.
- Willingness to use others to achieve aims.
- Lack of consideration and understanding for other people's feelings and desires.
- Arrogant or snobby behaviors and attitudes.

Narcissistic personality disorder (NPD) is a mental health illness in which individuals think they're better than everybody else. When many individuals have narcissistic traits, individuals with NPD have issues that affect their own lives, relationships and everyday life.

Individuals with NPD may seem arrogant, using an inflated self-image and disregard others' feelings. NPD is a part of this cluster of personality disorders with symptoms of extreme and unstable emotions and a twisted self-image. It normally begins in the early adult years and affects more men than women. Everyone is able to reveal narcissism from time to time --atmosphere self-important or not demonstrating compassion, or being greedy, aggressive, egocentric or insensitive.

In extreme circumstances, individuals may have a hierarchical character type, so they feel really entitled, but their behavior remains normal. An individual with NPD is significantly diminished. They may look too to other people to enhance their self-esteem can not feel compassion and have difficulty forming deep relationships.NPD is a psychological illness that affects every area of life, because symptoms are found during work and in your home. It can be difficult for other people to endure NPD symptoms, signifying that the victim becomes isolated. The distinction between NPD and normal narcissism is that NPD does not alter over time, and is not due to a health condition or medication. You do not grow from it, and it may lead to considerable distress.

Chapter 1 what's narcissistic personality disorder (NPD)?

The Term narcissism gets tossed around a lot within our Selfie-obsessed, celebrity-driven civilization, frequently to characterize somebody who appears overly vain or filled with these. But in emotional terms, narcissism does not mean self-explanatory --not of a real sort. It is more precise to state that individuals with narcissistic personality disorder (NPD) have been in love with the abysmal, grandiose images. And they are in love with this inflated self-image just because it permits them to steer clear of deep feelings of bitterness. But frees up their delusions of grandeur requires a great deal of work--and that is where the dysfunctional attitudes and behaviors arrive.

Narcissistic personality disorder involves a routine of ironically, arrogant thinking and behavior, a lack of compassion and consideration for other people, and an excessive need for respect. Others frequently explain people with NPD as cocky, manipulative, egotistical, condescending, and demanding. This thinking method and acting surfaces in each region of the narcissist's life: in the friendships and work to family and enjoy relationships.

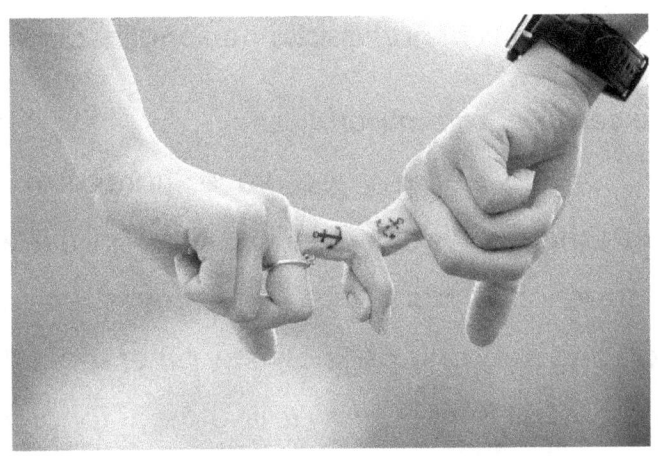

People with narcissistic personality disorder are very Resistant to changing their behavior, even if it is causing them difficulties. Their propensity is to turn the blame on to other people. What is more, they are very sensitive and react badly to the smallest criticisms, disagreements, or even perceived slights, which they see as personal attacks. For those men and women who live in the narcissist's life, it is often simpler just to go together with their requirements to get around the coldness and rages. But by knowing more about narcissistic personality disorder, you are able to spot the narcissists in your own life, shield yourself from their energy plays, and set healthier boundaries.

Signs and symptoms of narcissistic personality disorder

Grandiose sense of self-importance

Grandiosity is your defining feature of narcissism. Over simply arrogance or vanity, grandiosity is an unrealistic sense of superiority. Narcissists think they're unique or "particular" and may only be known by other special men and women. What is more, they're too great for anything ordinary or average. They simply wish to connect and participate with other high-status individuals, places, and items.

Narcissists also consider that they are better than everybody else Else and expect recognition as such-- even if they have done nothing to make it. They will frequently exaggerate or lie about their accomplishments and abilities. And if they talk about relationships or work, all you will hear is how much they bring, how good they are, and just how blessed the people in their own lives would be to own them. They're the most adorable star and everybody else is at best a little player.

Lives in a dream world that affirms their delusions of grandeur

Since reality does not encourage their grandiose opinion of themselves, narcissists reside in a dream world propped up by distortion, self-deception, and magical thinking. They twist self-glorifying fantasies of unlimited success, power, brilliance, beauty, and perfect love, making them feel unique and in management. These dreams shield them from feelings of inner emptiness and pity, so opinions and facts that contradict them are either ignored or rationalized away. Whatever threatens to explode the dream bubble is met with extreme defensiveness and even anger, therefore those around the narcissist learn how to tread carefully about their denial of fact.

Requires constant compliments and respect

A narcissist's feeling of excellence is just like a balloon that gradually loses air with no continuous flow of applause and recognition to help keep it inflated. The occasional compliment isn't sufficient. Narcissists need constant food for themselves to surround themselves with individuals who would like to cater to their own obsessive craving for affirmation. These relationships are incredibly one-sided. It is about what the admirer can perform to your narcissist, not the other way round. And if there's ever a disturbance or diminishment from the admirer's compliments and attention, the narcissist treats it as a betrayal.

Sense of entitlement

Since they consider themselves particular, narcissists anticipate Favorable treatment because of their thanks. They genuinely think that whatever they need, they ought to get. In addition they anticipate the people around them to automatically comply with their every desire and whim. That's their sole price. If you do not anticipate and fulfill their every demand, then you are useless. And in case you've got the guts to withstand their will or "selfishly" request something in return, then prepare yourself for aggression, outrage, or even the shoulder.

Exploits others without remorse or shame

Narcissists never acquire the capability to identify others' Feelings --to place themselves into other people's shoes. To put it differently, they lack compassion. In many ways, they see that the people in their own lives as items --there to serve their requirements. As a result, they do not think twice about taking advantage of others to achieve their own ends. Occasionally this social manipulation is malicious, but frequently it's just oblivious. Narcissists just don't consider how their behavior affects others. And if you point it out, they won't really get it. The one thing they know is their particular needs.

Often demeans, intimidates, bullies, or belittles other people

Narcissists feel threatened whenever they encounter a person who seems to get something they lack, trendy and confident people. They are also threatened by those who do not kowtow to them who challenge them at all. Their defense mechanisms are contempt. The only way to neutralize the danger and prop up their own sagging self would be to place those folks down. They can take action in a patronizing or dismissive manner, like to demonstrate how small another individual means. Or they might go on the assault with insults, name-calling, bullying, and risks to induce another person back online.

Do not fall for the dream

Narcissists can be pretty charming and magnetic. They're extremely good at developing a fantastical, flattering self-image that draws us. We are drawn to their evident confidence and exalted dreams--and also, the shakier our own self-esteem, the more enchanting the allure. It's easy to become trapped in their internet, believing that they'll meet our longing to feel more important and more living. Nonetheless, it's only a dream and a pricey one at that.

Your needs will not be fulfilled (or even recognized). It is important not to forget that narcissists are not searching for spouses; they're searching for obedient admirers. Your sole value into the narcissist is just as somebody who will tell them how good they are supposed to prop up their insatiable ego. Your needs and feelings do not count.

Have a look at how in which the narcissist treats others. If the Narcissist manipulates, hurts, lies and disrespects others, he or she'll finally treat you the exact same manner. Do not fall for the dream that you are different and will probably be spared.

Take the rose-colored eyeglasses. It is very important to see that the Narcissists in your life for whom they are, not that you need them to be. Quit making excuses for poor behavior or minimizing the damage it is causing you. Denial won't make it go away. The truth is that narcissists are extremely resistant to change, therefore the genuine question you have to ask yourself is if it is possible to live like this forever.

Concentrate on your personal fantasies. Rather than losing yourself at the Narcissist's delusions, concentrate on the things you need on your own. What do you wish to modify in your lifetime? What gifts do you want to grow? What dreams do you have to give up so as to make a more satisfying reality?

Set healthy boundaries

Healthy relationships are based on mutual esteem and caring. However, narcissists are not capable of true reciprocity in their relationships. It is not just they're not prepared; they aren't able. They do not see you. They do not hear you. They do not recognize you as somebody who is beyond their particular wants. As a result of this, narcissists frequently violate the bounds of others. What is more, they do this with a complete sense of entitlement. Narcissists believe nothing of moving borrowing or through your Possessions without inquiring, sifting through your email and private correspondence, eavesdropping on conversations, barging in without an invitation, stealing your thoughts, and providing you unwanted comments and guidance. They might even let you know exactly what to feel and think. It is very important to recognize these offenses for the things they are, which means that you may start to produce healthier boundaries wherever your requirements are respected.

Create a plan. If You've Got a long-standing routine of allowing other folks to violate your borders, it is not simple to return control. Set yourself up for success by meticulously considering your targets and the possible obstacles. Which are the most significant changes you would like to attain? Is there anything you have attempted previously together with the narcissist that functioned? Anything which has not? What's the balance of energy between you and how will that affect your strategy? How are you going to apply your new bounds? Answering these questions can allow you to evaluate your choices and create a realistic strategy.

Think about a gentle approach. If maintaining your connection Together with the narcissist is valuable to you, you'll need to tread gently. By pointing their hurtful or dysfunctional behavior, you're damaging their self-image of devotion. Attempt to send your message respectfully, and as softly as you can. Concentrate on how their behavior makes you feel, instead of on their motives and goals. Should they react to anger and defensiveness, try to stay calm. Walk away if need be and reevaluate the dialogue afterward.

Do not place a border unless you are prepared to keep it. You can rely on the narcissist to rebel against fresh boundaries and test your own limits, so be ready. Follow up with almost any impacts specified. If you back down, you send the message that you don't have to be taken seriously.

Be ready for different changes in the connection. The Narcissist will feel compromised and angry by your efforts to take charge of your lifetime. They're utilized to calling the shots. To compensate, they can step up their needs at different facets of the relationship, space themselves to punish you, or try to manipulate or appeal you into giving up the new bounds. It is your choice to stand firm.

Do not take things personally

To safeguard themselves from feelings of inferiority and Pity, narcissists should always deny their flaws, cruelties, and errors. Frequently, they'll do this by projecting their flaws onto others. It is very upsetting to have blamed for something that's not your fault or be characterized with adverse traits you do not have. However, as hard as it might be, try not to take it. It is actually not about you.

Do not buy in the narcissist's version of who you're Narcissists do not reside in reality, including their perspectives of different men and women. Do not let their pity and blame match endanger your self-esteem. Refuse to take undeserved responsibility, blame, or criticism. That negativity is the narcissists ' to maintain.

Do not argue with a narcissist. Once attacked, the organic Instinct is to safeguard yourself and demonstrate the narcissist's incorrect. But regardless of how logical you are or how to sound your debate, they are not likely to listen to you. And asserting the stage might increase the situation in a really disagreeable manner. Do not waste your breath. Just tell the narcissist you disagree with their evaluation, and then proceed.

Know yourself. The best shield against the insults and Projections of the narcissist is a powerful sense of self. When you understand your strengths and flaws, it is simpler to deny any unjust criticisms leveled against you.

Give up the need for acceptance. It is important to detach In the narcissist's view and any need to please or direct them at your cost. You have to be fine with understanding the facts on your own, even when a narcissist sees the problem differently.

Start Looking for purpose and support elsewhere

If you will remain in a relationship with a narcissist, be truthful with yourself about everything you can--and cannot --expect. A narcissist is not likely to transform into somebody who truly appreciates you, so you ought to appear elsewhere for psychological support and personal satisfaction.

Discover what healthy relationships see and feel just like. Should you come out of the real-life household, you might not have an excellent sense of exactly what a healthful give-and-take connection is. The narcissistic pattern of malfunction might feel comfortable to you. Just remind yourself that as comfortable as it seems, in addition, it makes you feel awful. In a mutual relationship, you may feel respected, listened to, and free to be yourself.

Spend some time with those that give you a fair reflection of that you are. To be able to keep perspective and prevent buying to the narcissist's distortions, it is important to spend some time with individuals who know you as you are and affirm your ideas and feelings.

Create new friendships, even if necessary, beyond the narcissist's orbit. Many narcissists isolate the men and women in their own lives to be able to manage them better. If that is the situation, you will want to spend some time rebuilding lapsed friendships or cultivating new connections.

Start Looking for significance and purpose at work, volunteering, and hobbies. Rather than looking into the narcissist to allow you to feel great on your own, pursue purposeful activities which make use of your abilities and permit you to contribute.

The Way to make a narcissist

Finish an abusive relationship isn't simple. Finish one Using a narcissist can be particularly difficult since they may be so charming and charismatic--at the onset of the connection or if you threaten to leave. It's easy to become jaded with the narcissist's manipulative behavior caught up in the necessity to find their acceptance, or perhaps to sense "gaslighted" and doubt your judgment. If you are codependent, your want to be faithful may trump your requirement to preserve your security and sense of self. Nonetheless, it's important to keep in mind that nobody deserves to be intimidated, threatened, or emotionally abused at a connection. There are means to escape the narcissist--along with the guilt and self-blame--and also start the recovery process yourself about narcissistic personality disorder. The more you know, the better you will have the ability to comprehend the techniques that a narcissist can utilize to help keep you at the connection. If you threaten to leave, a narcissist will frequently revive the flattery and adoration ("love bombing") that caused you to be curious about them in the first location. They will also make grand claims about altering their behavior that they don't intend to maintain down the reasons you are leaving. Becoming clear on the reason why you have to terminate the relationship might help keep you from being sucked back. Maintain your record someplace handy, like in your telephone, and refer to it if you are beginning to get self-doubts or the narcissist is putting on the charm or creating outlandish promises.

Seek support. During your time together, the narcissist may have ruined your relationships with family and friends or restricted your life. But regardless of your situation, you are not alone. Even in the event, you cannot reach out to older friends, you will find support from support groups or domestic violence helplines and shelters.

Do not make empty threats. It is a much better strategy to take the narcissist will not change and if you are ready, simply depart. Making risks or pronouncements will only forewarn the narcissist and also permit them to make it even more challenging for you to getaway.

To find out more about departing, read How to Escape an Abusive Relationship.

When you've left

Leaving a narcissist can be a massive blow to their awareness of entitlement and self-importance. Their enormous ego still has to be fed up, so they will often continue attempting to exert control on you. If allure and "love bombing" does not do the job, they can resort to threats, denigrating one to mutual acquaintances and friends, or depriving you, on societal networking or in person.

Cut off all contact with the narcissist. The contact you have together, the further hope you will give them , can reel you back in. It is safer to block their texts, calls, and emails, and even disconnect from them on interpersonal networking. In case you have children together, have others along with you for any scheduled custody handovers.

Let yourself grieve. Breakups can be extremely debilitating, whatever the conditions. Even finishing a poisonous connection will leave you feeling depressed, angry, perplexed, and mourning the lack of shared responsibilities and dreams. Healing can take some time, so go easy on you and turn to relatives and friends for assistance.

Do not anticipate the narcissist to talk about your grief. After the Message sinks so you may no more be feeding yourself, the narcissist will soon move to exploit somebody else. They will not feel guilt or loss, just that endless demand for admiration and compliments. That is no reflection on you, but instead an example of how really one-sided their relationships consistently are.

If you want aid for narcissistic personality disorder

Because of this disease's nature, people with NPD Are unwilling to admit they have a problem and are much more reluctant to seek assistance. When they do, a narcissistic personality disorder can be quite hard to take care of. But that does not mean there is no hope or changes are not possible. Mood stabilizers, antidepressants, and antipsychotic drugs are sometimes prescribed in severe cases or in case you're NPD co-occur with a different disease. But, ordinarily psychotherapy is the principal type of therapy.

Working with a skilled therapist, you can Learn How to take responsibility for the activities, develop a greater sense of proportion, and develop healthy relationships. You might even focus on developing your emotional intelligence (EQ). EQ is the capacity to comprehend, utilize, and handle your own emotions in positive approaches to interact with other people, communicate effectively, and build powerful relationships. Significantly, the abilities which make up emotional intelligence can be learned at any given moment.

Narcissistic personality disorder (NPD) is a character Disorder where individuals have an inflated view of themselves. In addition they have an extreme demand for the admiration and care of others.

Individuals with NPD Might Are generally unhappy and frustrated when they are not given the compliments or special favors they deserve. Others might find them as snobbish and arrogant, and might not like being around them.

NPD can lead to difficulties in several Regions of life, such as:
- Work
- College
- Relationships

However, the disease can be handled with talk therapy and certain lifestyle enhancements.

Identifying narcissistic personality disorder traits
Individuals with NPD are often portrayed as being the following:
- Arrogant
- Self-centered
- demanding

They frequently have large self-esteem and Might believe they're Exceptional or special in comparison to other individuals. But they appear to need excessive compliments and esteem, and they might respond poorly to perceived criticism.

Narcissists also often exaggerate their particular abilities and Achievements, while downplaying those others. They are normally obsessed with power, achievement, and attractiveness. They may even take part in impulsive behaviors, such as risky sex and gaming.

Some characteristics of NPD may seem like optimism. But, healthful confidence and NPD is not the exact same thing.

Individuals who have healthy self-esteem are often modest, while individuals with NPD rarely are. They are inclined to place themselves on a base and perceive themselves as better than everybody else.

Indicators of narcissistic personality disorder

NPD generally appears in early maturity. Individuals with the Disease might not recognize they have an issue as it goes contrary to their self-image. You might have NPD if:
- You come across as pretentious and boastful, inducing other people to prevent you
- Your relationships are unfulfilling

- You become miserable, upset, and perplexed when things do not go away
- You've ongoing problems together:
○ work
○ college
○ relationships
○ financing
○ alcohol
○ medication

If You Think you own NPD, schedule an appointment with your physician or a mental health specialist. They could decide if you Have this character disorder and recommend remedies to help deal with symptoms.

Physicians and mental health professionals Frequently use the Newest edition of the Diagnostic and Statistical Manual of Mental Disorders (DSM-5), Relereleasedthe American Psychiatric Association, to diagnose Psychological disorders, for Example NPD. The DSM-5 diagnostic criteria for NPD comprise the following characteristics:

- With an inflated sense of self-importance and entitlement
- needing continuous admiration and compliments

- expecting special treatment because of perceived excellence
- exaggerating accomplishments and abilities
- responding negatively to criticism
- being obsessed with dreams about power, achievement, and attractiveness
- benefiting from others
- With an inability or unwillingness to comprehend the needs and feelings of other Men and Women
- behaving in an arrogant manner

To ascertain if you satisfy these standards, your physician or mental health professional may ask you to complete a questionnaire. You could also be analyzed for other psychological ailments and health conditions.

Reasons for narcissistic personality disorder

The causes of NPD are not well known. But, inherited genetic defects are considered to be responsible for several instances of NPD. Contributing environmental variables may include:
- Youth abuse or neglect
- Excessive parental pampering
- Unrealistic expectations from parents
- Physical promiscuity (frequently exerts narcissism)
- Cultural influences

Remedy for narcissistic personality disorder

Remedy for NPD chiefly contains talk therapy, also called psychotherapy. If NPD indications happen along with depression or another mental health illness, then proper medications might be employed when treating another ailment. But, there are no drugs to take care of NPD.

Talk therapy can help you learn how to relate better to other people so that your relationships can be pleasurable, romantic, and more rewarding. Creating positive connections with other individuals is able to greatly improve a variety of regions of your own life. Talk therapy also can show You the Way to:

- enhance your cooperation with co-workers and peers
- keep your personal relationships
- recognize your strengths and possible so you can endure criticisms or failures
- know and handle your emotions
- Deal with any self-esteem Difficulties
- set realistic targets for yourself

Take all of your treatment sessions and take some medicines as directed. With time, you will start to see a difference in your own relationships with other people.

The next lifestyle remedies might help you while you proceed through treatment.

• Prevent alcohol, drugs, and other chemicals that activate negative behaviors

• Exercise at least three times a week to help enhance mood.

• Engage in comfort methods, such as meditation and yoga, to decrease tension and anxiety.

Retrieval from narcissistic personality disorder takes time. Stay inspired by maintaining your restoration goals in mind and reminding yourself that you're able to operate to fix damaged relationships to maybe become more satisfied with your own life.

What is the prognosis for somebody with rea a personality disorder?

The advantages of therapy may change based upon the intensity of your symptoms and your willingness to devote yourself to therapy.

However, symptoms of NPD generally improve as time passes. Should motivated and actively work toward change, you will probably have the ability to mend damaged relationships and be more fulfilled with your daily life.

Living together with narcissistic personality disorder

Even though it can be difficult to take care of narcissistic character disorder, it is possible to work through it. Seeing a therapist or psycho counseling can be quite helpful, as can changing how you think and socialize with other people daily.

Bear in mind that you're in behavior, and you may change it at any given moment.

What Are the Nine Traits of a Narcissist?

Narcissistic personality disorder (NPD), or narcissism, is a personality disorder characterized by a feeling of grandiosity, the demand for admiration and attention, shallow social relations along with a lack of empathy. It frequently accompanies other psychiatric ailments and can be tricky to deal with.

Nine Signs and Symptoms of Narcissism

Symptoms -- known as core attributes -- of narcissistic character disorder (narcissism) contain:

1. Grandiosity
O Exaggerated sense of self-importance
O Feeling superior to other people and deserve special treatment
O Feelings are usually accompanied by fantasies of unlimited success, brilliance, strength, beauty, or enjoy

2. Excessive demand for respect
O has to be the middle of focus
O Frequently monopolize conversations
O Patients feel slighted, abused, depleted, and enraged when dismissed

3. Superficial and exploitative relationships
O Relationships derive from surface features rather than the exceptional qualities of others
O People are just valued only to the extent that they are seen as beneficial

4. Deficiency of compassion

O Severely restricted or totally lacking capability to take care of the psychological needs or experiences of the others, even loved ones

5. Identity disturbance

O Sense of self is extremely superficial, exceptionally stiff, and frequently fragile

O Self-stability is dependent on keeping up the opinion that you is exceptional

O Grandiose sense of self is readily jeopardized

O Patients escape from or deny truths that challenge grandiosity

6. Difficulty with dependence and attachment

O Relies on comments from the environment

O Relationships just exist to shore up favorable self-image

O Interactions are shallow

O Intimacy is averted

7. Persistent feelings of emptiness and boredom

O When compliments and attention aren't available, patients feel empty, tired, depressed, or nervous

8. Vulnerability to life alterations

O Difficulty maintaining reality-based professional and personal goals as time passes

O Compromises demanded by college, tasks, and associations might feel excruciating

O Young adults might have a "failure to start"

9. Narcissistic personality disorder is also a substantial risk factor for suicide and suicidal attempts.

What's Narcissism Diagnosed?

Narcissistic personality disorder (narcissism) is diagnosed with The Diagnostic and Statistical Manual of Mental Disorders (DSM-5) standards) someone must meet five of the next traits to get a diagnosis of narcissistic personality disorder.

1. A grandiose sense of self-importance
2. Preoccupation with fantasies of unlimited success, power, brilliance, beauty, or ideal love
3. Belief He or she is "special" and unique and can only be known by or should associate with, other special or high-status individuals or associations
4. requires excessive admiration
5. Has a sense of entitlement
6. Is interpersonally exploitative -- makes the most of other people

7. Lacks empathy

8. Envies others or thinks others are envious of their

9. Shows arrogant, behavior and attitudes

What Is the Treatment for Narcissism?

Remedy for narcissistic personality disorder (narcissism) may be difficult but treatment can often assist. Kinds of therapy include:

• Supportive psychotherapy that utilizes both psychodynamic cognitive-behavioral methods, frequently combined with psychopharmacologic control

• Structured psychotherapies

O Mentalization-based treatment

Patients are educated to self-reflect

O Transference-focused psychotherapy

Identifies patient's therapy Objectives and established a remedy contract between patient and therapist

O Schema-focused psychotherapy

Uses cognitive-behavioral treatment, attachment theory, and psychodynamic treatment to deal with negative senses of self, other people, and of the place on Earth which are established in ancient life

O Dialectical behavioral treatment

A cognitive-behavioral treatment (CBT) that unites individual treatment with group therapy has core fundamentals of approval and change

Medicines may also be used when treating narcissistic personality disorder, especially in patients with acute symptoms and might be a threat to others or self, and patients with other, treatable psychiatric problems.

Medicines that may be used to Deal with narcissistic character disorder include:

- Mood stabilizers
- Antidepressants
- Antipsychotics
- Kinds of Narcissists

They generally think they're superior to other people and therefore are eligible for special treatment. They display a pervading pattern of grandiosity occasionally in behavior, and sometimes just in dreams of success and electricity. Beneath the surface, they don't enjoy themselves (which I think means they are incapable of loving anybody else). They're driven by pity, have a continuous need for respect, and will go to great lengths to protect their delicate egos, using their coping mechanisms being abusive. Last, and possibly the most famous symptom of this disease, is their blatant lack of compassion for others.

Now, because a single narcissist can present quite differently compared to another, I decided to scour the net searching for information on how to categorize different kinds of narcissists that walk among people, and there appeared to be a vast selection of phrases used, occasionally to explain precisely the exact same pattern, which adds to the confusion surrounding this under-studied type of personality disorder. But, I eventually stumbled upon a post written by Kristen Milstead, a Ph.D. in Sociology that lay all these miscellaneous terms I'd encounter out superbly in a manner that made complete sense.

Types

Scientists have identified four chief types of narcissists, each demonstrating different behavior to secure their delicate inner core sense of self. Within each one of these three kinds are just six sub-types that describe the way the traits might seem to other people.

It's also important to remember that these various kinds are generalizations, rather than every narcissist will fit neatly into a single category. Just like everything in existence, there are always shades of gray and a narcissist can cross more than 1 type.

Vintage

Vintage narcissists are the normal narcissists who most men and women consider when they hear the expression "narcissist", also called high-functioning, exhibitionistic, or grandiose narcissists. They exhibit attention-seeking behavior about their accomplishments, feel entitled to special treatment and expect other people to bow down and kiss their own feet. They aren't interested in anybody but themselves and get easily bored when the conversation turns from them. They tend to perceive themselves prior to most people, but paradoxically are distressed to feel significant.

Vulnerable

The second significant kind of narcissist is that the exposed narcissist, also occasionally called brittle, compensatory or cupboard narcissists. Like the basic narcissists they feel superior to the majority of people they match; nevertheless, they're more introverted and hate being in the middle of attention. They like to attach themselves to particular individuals rather than seeking the distinctive treatment themselves. They're more inclined to seek out shame others or flatter and suck up to other people, sometimes through extreme generosity, simply to get the attention and respect they want to enhance their awareness of self-worth.

Communal

The third significant sort of narcissist is that the communal narcissist. This kind is a bit more difficult to see at first glance since they concentrate on promoting themselves through their devotion to other people, communal objectives, and also their self-proclaimed super-ability to listen to and socialize with other people. They will frequently contribute to charities (or brag about how little they spend on themselves) and volunteer their time "helping" others. They may chat about their "life's assignment" in grandiose phrases or dedicate themselves to the effect that will "change the world".

Even though they seem unprofessional about the outside, dig a bit deeper and you could realize they are hugely territorial of their charity they function and far more worried about getting a pat in the back because they participated in place of the communal goal they're allegedly working toward. The fact of the matter is they are merely involved in the neighborhood to confirm their sorely lacking feeling of self.

Malignant

The fourth and final significant kind of narcissist is that the cancerous, or poisonous, narcissist. They're highly manipulative and exploit others (generally for enjoyment). These narcissists often exhibit paranoia and antisocial traits not present in timeless, vulnerable, or communal narcissists. They may be ruthless in their principal wish to dominate and control others. They are deceptive and competitive. Worse yet they lack guilt for their activities.

Sub-Type 1: Overt vs. Covert

As I mentioned previously, all these significant kinds of narcissists comprise sub-types that describe the way the traits might seem to other people. The very first sub-type clarifies how the narcissist uses to receive their needs fulfilled...Are they overt and use theatres that are apparent and from the open for everyone to see? Or are they covert and utilize techniques that are stealthier and much more secretive? As an instance, most of us recognize that narcissists prefer to provide insults and put down people. An overt narcissist can do this in clear and unmistakable ways, even though a covert narcissist can do this in much more passive-aggressive manners. A covert narcissist can control others without them knowing they had been manipulated, or their strategies permit them to deny what occurred.

Vintage and tropical narcissists are almost always obvious, and vulnerable narcissists are almost always secret; nonetheless, in regards to malignant narcissists...they could be.

Sub-Type 2: Somatic vs. Cerebral

The next sub-type defines exactly what the narcissist worth most in him or her as well as others. No narcissist wishes to be out-shined with their spouse. Their spouse is seen more like a glistening object they could show off to boost their own social standing. This sub-type includes somatic narcissists that are obsessed with their own bodies and their outside appearance and cerebral narcissists that encounter as know-it-alls. They see themselves as the smartest ones inside the room and just like to attempt to impress folks with their achievements. One of the four main kinds of narcissists -- classic, vulnerable, temperate or cancerous -- may be somatic or cerebral.

Sub-Type 3: Inverted vs. Sadistic

The final and last sub-type includes a few unique kinds of narcissists. The first special sub-type is that the inverted narcissist applies to exposed, covert narcissists. This group of narcissists is codependent and tends to attach themselves to other narcissists to feel unique. They tend to get a victim mindset and also endure child abandonment problems.

The next specific sub-type is that the sadistic narcissist...that a distinctive sort of malignant narcissist. This group resembles sociopaths and psychopaths because they take great joy in others' pain. They enjoy humiliating and damaging people, and at times have bizarre physical fetishes.

Since I adore visuals, I put together the next info-graphic so you can view how the kinds and sub-types are all interrelated:

Reasons

Now that we have reviewed the 10 distinct kinds of narcissists, let us take a peek at just what the hell causes this character disorder. There's a good deal of speculation on the market, but the truth of this is that nobody actually knows. But, I did find two distinct formal concepts with this one...the very first developed by Otto Kernberg and the next by Heinz Kohut.

I would like to begin by stating that kids are inherently narcissistic...and this is totally normal. External influences govern their self-esteem and they want other people to respect them so as to feel great about them. Therefore, the reason we, as parents, offer positive reinforcement to our kids.

Based on Kernberg, acquiring an unempathetic and distant mother who's hypercritical and devalues her kid induces the child to make an internalized grandiose self as a defense mechanism against the perceived shortage of love and consequent psychological injury. He speculated that NPD is a pathological improvement.

On the other hand, Kohut felt that the environment is the significant reason and that NPD has been caused by arrested development in ordinary psychological development.

Now, I am not a psychologist; nonetheless I have rubbed elbows with a lot of individuals who exhibit real personality traits in my own time, and I can confidently state I have met some who have certainly had an upbringing in a house with a very unempathetic mother. On the flip side, I've fulfilled narcissistic men and women who also have apparently "ordinary" moms and had more of a latch-key kind of youth. The frequent thread from my standpoint seems to be among those kids not getting their emotional needs met, whether that's via a hypercritical parent or a neglectful parent.

At the end of the afternoon, it appears that there is agreement that some of the risk factors in early youth include:

- Insensitive parenting,
- Inconsistent or negligent care,
- Excess criticism,
- Abuse,
- Trauma,
- Extremely Substantial expectations, and
- Over-praising and surplus bloat, when parents concentrate heavily on the child's look or special talent (generally due to their lack of self-esteem).

There's also speculation that abnormalities in an individual's genes might impact the link between their mind and their behaviors.

Warning Signs

So...what are the warning signals you might be in the existence of, or even worse, at a connection with a narcissistic man?

Well, there are lots of outward signs which should make your Spidey senses tingling...

Initially, they may encounter as incredibly charming and likable. You know...that person you couldn't wait to watch again since they made you feel good?

But if you dig a little deeper you might just notice that they
- Always bring the conversation back to them,
- Often brag about their skills or achievements,
- prefer to name-drop,
- are really quite shallow and therefore are not able to really be exposed...there is not any such thing as a profound conversation with a real narcissist.

- tend to fish for praise Due to Their exaggerated requirement for validation,
- can become aggressive when criticized...even with constructive criticism,
- are perfectionistic,
- prefer to one-up everyone because they see themselves as exceptional,
- might not follow the principles Due to Their feeling of entitlement,
- are incapable of self-reflection and not able to take responsibility for their actions. They prefer to play the "blame game".
- are control freaks, so that they tend not to communicate quite well and certainly do not function within a group,
- Possess a clear lack of compassion for the others, they don't understand the significance of the term "to place yourself in somebody else's shoes".
- Might be too critical of the others,
- lack bounds, within the sense of entitlement,
- have a good deal of superficial friends, possibly on their social networking account nonetheless, they seriously lack in long-term or close friendships or associations.

- in general, they simply leave a wake of wreckage behind them where they go...make it a set of broken friendships, romantic relationships that went badly wrong, or dreadful work experiences.

These are a few of the outward indications you might be coping with a real-life person; nonetheless, I would like to dig a bit deeper and examine a few of the inward signs we actually have to be watching out for. To put it differently, the way they make us feel.

As I mentioned previously, a narcissistic person will cause you to feel really special at the start of your relationship. They could shower you with compliments, or simply take you on great adventures. They'll make you feel so great you might just ignore a few of these warning signals.

You might even begin to make excuses for their bad behavior..."he should have just had a lousy moment." Or..." wow, that individual must have hurt her." Or you might even take it on yourself..."I must have misunderstood."

Once you are completely drawn in, the narcissist in your life will begin changing this up and eventually become manipulative. It'll be subtle at first, but over time, you are going to begin doubting yourself and might even end up living in a fog of confusion. You will feel as if you aren't good enough and can not do anything right. Your self-esteem is going to be stripped off and you'll be forever walking on eggshells trying to appease the man or woman who once made you feel exceptionally unique.

If you're worried you could be stuck into a relationship with or are working with a narcissistic ex that's endangering your own children, I invite you to achieve out to assist

Different types Of Narcissists & the Way to Motivate Them

People today appear to be fascinated with the idea of narcissism. Maybe it is because we are a bit narcissistic or know somebody else who's. However, before you jump to tag someone, a narcissist considers that there are different kinds of narcissism. While all of them maintain the core features of narcissism (entitlement, lack of compassion, and a demand for management), they are exhibited through different behavior changes in the level of seriousness and danger.

Just how various kinds of narcissism are you?

Even though someone could be identified with narcissistic personality disorder (NPD), there's absolutely no clinical investigation for almost any subtypes of narcissism. Some kinds of narcissism are identified and super- reviewed studies, whereas other forms have been named and popularized by different health professionals. Thus, there's absolutely no definite amount of millennial subtypes.

1. Healthful narcissism

Yes, healthful narcissism exists. To begin with, just because somebody has narcissistic traits does not mean that they have narcissistic stick personality disorder. According to the Diagnostic and Statistical Manual (DSM-5), to become clinically diagnosed with NPD, an individual has to display at least 55 percent of the most typical narcissism indications. Lots of men and women might have traits of narcissism without fulfilling the standards for the disease. Wholesome narcissism is a type of its own and is really positive.

2. Grandiose narcissism

Grandiose narcissism closely resembles the wider comprehension of what creates a narcissist. In psychology, grandiosity describes using an unrealistic sense of superiority. Hence, grandiose narcissism involves overestimating one's skill promising dominance over other people and using a normally inflated sense of self-esteem. This Sort of narcissism has been Examined and validated through reviewed studies often in opposition to vulnerable narcissism (also called covert narcissism).

"Grandiose narcissism is if a person's narcissistic Attributes --entitlement, braggadocio, and self-obsession--have been publicly displayed, frequently at the cost of other people," Neo states. Grandiose narcissists may be magical but often lack compassion. In discussions, they do not relate to individuals, Neo describes, but instead one-up them. This is because they crave attention, like watching others confused and hurt, or even both.

When coping with a grandiose narcissist, or any Kind of Narcissist for this thing, it is important to place boundaries. "Know that you can be assertive at precisely the exact same time," Neo states. "They'll push your boundaries, eroding them a lesser degree of therapy becomes the new standard. Be ready to apply your borders --much better, walk-off."

3. Vulnerable narcissism, also Called covert narcissism

Covert narcissism can also be called vulnerable narcissism. In Resistance into the grandiose narcissists, these people today are inclined to be bashful and self-effacing. According to the American Journal of Psychiatry (AJP), the "covert subtype is inhibited, manifestly desperate, hypersensitive to the tests of others while envious." They crave people's recognition and get really defensive in the face of criticism.

4. Malignant narcissism

Malignant narcissists, exactly like the title suggests, are Malicious and manipulative. They reveal signs of sadism and aggression, and based on AJP, would be the most acute subtype of narcissistic character disorder.

5. Physical narcissism

Physical narcissists "possess an exceedingly optimistic, Egotistical admiration of their physical prowess," couples' therapist Brandon Santan, Ph.D., informs mind body green. "They could become absorbed with their own obsession with physical functionality and also the demand for the physical esteem of others"

Physical narcissists tend to be serial cheaters, use gender to Heal individuals, and might behave violently through intercourse. To protect yourself from this sort of narcissist, your safest choice is to escape the relationship and seek treatment that will assist you get through the separation with a narcissist.

Physical narcissism is part of a three-part narcissism typing System that includes physical narcissism, somatic narcissism, and cerebral narcissism. Not one of them is supported by study, but the machine gained some fame as some psychological health professionals rely on these to further categorize various kinds of narcissism.

6. Somatic narcissism

Somatic narcissists derive their self-worth in their bodies. Psychotherapist Christine Scott-Hudson, LMFT, writes, "This will manifest as somebody feeling beautiful, stronger, or fitter than many others."

Somatic narcissists often obsess over their weight and Physical look and criticize others according to their look. They generally ignore the demands of others and reevaluate their own. If you are coping with you, Scott-Hudson states, "prevent displaying psychological responses to their behavior because narcissists feed drama."

7. Cerebral narcissist

Cerebral or intellectual narcissists derive their Self-importance in their heads compared to the somatic narcissist who participates worth in their bodies. "Cerebral narcissists receive their source from feeling brighter, smarter, and much more intelligent than other people," Scott-Hudson informs mind body green.

8. Spiritual narcissist

Spiritual narcissists frequently use their spirituality Justify destructive behaviors and utilize religious jargon to intimidate other people, Neo describes. "You see, the narcissist should project an idealized version of himself to escape his broken, insecure self," she states, and religious narcissists use apparently sensitive and religious acts as a means to elevate themselves over others.

Neo says young people or Those Who Have undergone Important upheavals, like a movement or even a divorce, are more vulnerable to these religious narcissists' "attractive, lively influence." If someone you know uses their spirituality as a tool to control or belittle you, then different from them.

Narcissism is present on a spectrum, and you will find lots of various kinds of narcissism, some which are more stressing than others. If you are dealing with a person who you suspect could have real personality disorder, the best thing to do to protect yourself is to put strong boundaries and walk away in the connection entirely.

Chapter 2 Narcissistic abuse chief facets?

What's Verbal Abuse? The Way to Recognize Abusive Behavior and Things to Do Next

Abuse comes in many forms, not all of which can be bodily. When somebody uses words to demean, frighten, or restrain someone, it is deemed verbal abuse.

You will hear about verbal abuse from the context of a Romantic connection or even a parent-child relationship. However, it may also happen in other family relationships, socially, or at work.

If you are being abused, know that it is not your fault. Keep on reading to find out more, such as understanding it and what you could do next.

What is the distinction between verbal abuse and also abnormal' argument?

Most of us get into debates from time to time. Occasionally we lose our cool and shout. It is all a part of being human. But verbal abuse is not normal.

The problem is, even Once You are involved in a verbally abusive Connection, it could wear you down and look normal to you.

Here are some examples of what regular disagreements seem like:

- They do not split into name-calling or individual attacks.
- They do not happen daily.
- Arguments revolve around a fundamental matter. They are not character assassinations.
- You Listen and attempt to comprehend the other's place, even if you're furious.
- One of you may shout or say something genuinely awful from frustration, but it is an unusual phenomenon and you work together.
- Even if you can not agree, you are in a position to compromise or proceed without punishments or dangers.
- Arguments are not a zero-sum sport: One individual will not win in the detriment of another.

Think about it a red flag if another person participates in these behaviors:

- They Insult or try to humiliate you. They then accuse you of being too sensitive or state it was a joke and you don't have any sense of humor.
- They frequently shout or shout.
- Arguments take you by surprise, however you get blamed for them.

- The First debate sets off a series of accusations and dredging up of insignificant problems to set you on the protection.
- They attempt to cause you to feel guilty and place themselves as the sufferer.
- They conserve their hurtful behaviors for when you are alone but behave entirely different when others are about.
- They get into your own personal space or prevent you from going away.
- They struck the wall, pound their fists, or throw items.
- They need Charge for not having strike you.

1. Name-calling

Whether it's a romantic affair, a parent-child relationship, or even the bully on the playground, name-calling is unhealthy. Occasionally evident, sometimes disguised as "pet names" or "teasing," Habitual name-calling is a way of belittling you.

As an instance:

- "You do not get it, sweetie, because you are just too dumb."
- "It is no Wonder everybody says you are a jerk."

2. Condescension

Condescension is just another effort to belittle you. The Abuser's opinions can be amusing, disdainful, and patronizing. It is all to make they feel superior.

As an instance:

- "Allow me to see if I will put this in simple terms that even you can understand."
- "I am positive You place a great deal of work in your cosmetics, but go wash it off before somebody sees you."

3. Criticism

There is nothing wrong with constructive criticism. But in a verbally abusive relationship, it is especially persistent and harsh in an effort to chip away in the self-esteem.

As an instance:

- "You Are always mad about something, always playing the victim. That is why nobody likes you."
- "You Screwed up . Cannot you do anything right?"

4. Degradation

Abusers would like you to feel terrible about yourself. They use Humiliation and shame to irritate you and eat away at your confidence.

As an instance:

- "Before I Came you're nothing. Without me you will be nothing."
- "I mean, Look on your own. Who would like you?"

5. Manipulation

Manipulation is an effort to cause you to do something without which makes it a direct purchase. Make no mistake about it: It is intended to restrain you and keep you off-balance.

As an instance:

- "Should you do this, it demonstrates that you don't care for your own loved ones and everybody will understand it."
- "You would do this for me if you really loved me"

6. Blame

We are all responsible for something once in a while. But a Verbally abusive individual blames you for their behavior. They would like you to feel that you just bring verbal abuse on your own.

As an instance:

- "I despise Getting into fights; however, you make me so angry!"
- "I've to yell, as you are so ridiculous and thickheaded!"

7. Accusations

If someone is repeatedly telling you of items, they are jealous or envious. Or maybe they are the one guilty of the behavior. In any event, it can cause you to wonder whether you are doing something improper.

As an instance:

- "I watched how you looked at them. You cannot tell me nothing is happening there."
- "Why cannot you give me your mobile phone if you have got nothing to hide?"

8. Withholding or isolation

Refusing to Speak with you, look you in the eye, or perhaps maintain exactly the exact same room with you're intended to allow you to work harder to get their attention.

As an instance:

- In a Friend's home, you do or say something that they do not like. Without a word they storm outside and sit in the vehicle, leaving one to describe and say farewell to your hosts.
- They understand You have to communicate about who is picking up the children, but they refuse to respond to your texts or calls.

9. Gaslighting

Gaslighting is a systematic attempt to force you to question your own version of events. It can cause you to apologize for things which are not your own fault. In addition, it can make you dependent on the abuser.

As an instance:

- You remember an occasion, arrangement, or debate as well as the abuser denies it occurred at all. They might tell you it is all in your head, you guessed it, or are making this up.
- They inform other people that you are forgetful or have psychological issues to repaint the illusion.

10. Circular arguments

It is not uncommon for 2 people to disagree or argue about The exact same thing over once till they find common ground. But abusers will reignite that old debate over and over simply to push your buttons without planning to meet at the center.

As an instance:

- Your job Requires one to place in overtime with no notice. Each time it happens, the debate on your tardiness starts afresh.
- You have made it very clear that you are not prepared for children, but your spouse brings it up each month.

11. Hazards

Outright risks can signify that verbal abuse may grow. They are intended to frighten you into compliance.

As an instance:

- "If you Come home tonight, you may come across that a 'for sale' sign on the yard, and that I might only be gone with the children."
- "Should you Do that, nobody would blame me for the way I would respond."

What to do

If you believe you are experiencing verbal abuse, then trust your instincts. Remember there is a possibility it will gradually escalate. Now that you realize it, you need to determine how you are going to do something about it.

There is no single answer for everything to do. A lot is dependent on your unique conditions.

Reasoning using an aide is tempting, but unlikely to operate. Bear in mind, you're not liable for someone else's behavior.

However, you may set boundaries. Start refusing to participate in unreasonable arguments. Inform them you are going to no longer react to overlook verbal abuse.

Limit your exposure to the gardener as far as you can. If you travel at the same social circles, you may need to make some tough choices. If you can not prevent the individual completely, try to keep it down to scenarios where other people are around.

Then, once you're prepared, cut all ties in the event that you're able to. Breaking Things off with your abuser can be challenging in certain circumstances, like in the event that you live together, have kids with each other, or are reliant on these in some manner.

You may find it helpful to speak with a counselor or join a Support group. Sometimes a person's view can help you see things in a brand new light and determine exactly what to do.

The Way to Spot and Respond to Emotional Blackmail

What is the definition?

Emotional blackmail refers to a style of manipulation in which someone uses your emotions as a means to control your behavior or convince you to see things their way.

How it works

Like average blackmail, psychological blackmail involves someone attempting to get what they need from you. But rather than holding keys contrary to you personally, they control you with your own emotions.

Based on Forward, psychological blackmail progresses through six specific phases:

1. Demand

The very first phase of emotional blackmail entails a demand.

The person may say this explicitly:"I do not believe you should hang out with so anymore."

2. Resistance

If you do not wish to do exactly what they need, they will likely Push.

You may say right, "You are not insured, therefore I am not Comfortable allowing you to drive my car"

But if you worry how they will have a flat refusal, then you may resist more discreetly by:
- "forgetting" To put petrol in the vehicle
- neglecting to leave your keys
- saying nothing and hoping they overlook

3. Stress

Individuals still say wants and needs in healthful relationships. In an ordinary connection, as soon as you express immunity, another individual normally responds by falling the problem or making an attempt to discover a solution together.

A blackmailer will force you to fulfill their need, possibly with many distinct approaches, such as:

- replicating their requirement in a means which makes them look great (e.g.,"I am only considering their future")
- list Manners your immunity negatively influences them
- saying Things such as, "If you loved me, you would do it"
- criticizing or demeaning you

4. Hazards

Emotional blackmail can entail direct or indirect dangers:

- Immediate threat. "Should you go out with friends and family tonight, I will not be here when you return."
- Indirect threat. "If you cannot remain with me tonight once I want you, perhaps somebody else will."

They May also mask a risk as a favorable guarantee:"If you stay home tonight, we will have a far better time than you would have really going out. This is essential for our connection."

While this does not look like much of a threat, they are still attempting to control you. While they do not clearly state the consequences of your denial, they do suggest continued immunity will not help your connection.

5. Compliance

You do not need them to make well on their risks, So that you give up and give in. You may wonder if their "petition" even justified your immunity.

Compliance May Be an ultimate procedure, since they wear you down over time with risks and pressure. As soon as you devote, madness gives way to peace. They have what they desire, so they may seem especially loving and kind -- for now.

6. Repetition

When you show another person you will eventually concede, they know precisely how to play similar scenarios later on.

During the years, the procedure of psychological blackmail educates you that it is a lot easier to comply than confront persistent pressure and risks. You might come to accept their love is something they will withhold before you agree together.

They Might Even learn that a Specific kind of danger will get the work done quicker. Because of this, this routine will likely continue.

Frequent examples

While emotional blackmailers frequently use a mix of Tactics, Forward indicates their behaviors normally align with one of four chief styles:

Punishers

Someone with punishment strategies will state what they desire and then inform you exactly what will happen if you do not comply.

This frequently means direct risks, but punishers additionally use Aggression, anger, or quiet treatment to control.

Here is 1 case to think about:

Your spouse comes up and kisses you as you walk in.

"I left a massive sale now! Let us celebrate. Dinner, dance, Love..." they say with a suggestive wink.

"Congratulations!" You state. "But I am exhausted. I had intended to have a long bath and unwind. How about tomorrow?"

Their mood changes immediately. They sulk down the hallway, slamming doors as they go. If you follow and attempt to speak to them, they refuse to react.

Self-punishers

This sort of emotional blackmail also entails risks. Rather than threatening you, nevertheless, self-punishers describe how your immunity will hurt them

- "Should you won't give me money, I'm likely to lose my car"
- "Should you do not let's live with you, we are going to be homeless. Think about your nephews! Who knows what's going to happen with them? Would you need to live with this?"

Individuals using self-punishment approaches may spin the Circumstance To make it look like their issues are the fault so as to allow you to feel much more likely to take responsibility and help them.

Sufferers

A victim will frequently express their feelings.

If they think you have slighted them want you to perform something for these, they might say nothing and reveal their unhappiness with expressions of:

- Sadness or dejection, such as frowns, sighs, tears, or moping
- Pain or Distress

Nevertheless, They May also give you a complete rundown of everything leading to their distress.

As an instance:

Last week, you said to your friend that you wanted to locate A roommate to get the bare bedroom and attached bath. Your buddy explained, "Why not allow me to stay there at no cost?" You laughed off the comment, believing it was a joke.

Tantalizers

Some Kinds of emotional blackmail appear more like type gestures.

A tantalizer holds wages over your mind so as to get something out of you, offering encouragement and compliments. But every moment you pass one barrier, there is another waiting. You can not keep up.

The Way to respond to this

If you guess you are on the receiving end of psychological Blackmail, there are a couple of things that you can do in order to react productively.

Some People today learn blackmail tactics (such as guilt excursions) from Parents, grandparents, or previous partners. These behaviors become a constant way of Getting needs fulfilled, Myers describes.

Nevertheless, others May intentionally use Psychological blackmail. If you do not feel secure facing the individual, you might choose to bypass these (more about which to do in this situation later).

First, recognize what is not emotional blackmail

When a loved one's wants or bounds activate frustration or distress, you might choose to resist.

But, everyone has the right to communicate and restate Boundaries if required. It's only psychological blackmail when it entails stress, threats, and attempts to control you. Myers also clarifies that projecting memories and feelings of Past experiences are able to affect a current scenario look like blackmail.

"If we react to someone from insecurity or fear -- Believing that saying holding a border will cause rejection -- that may feel as emotional blackmail. But, that may be an erroneous projection of what could really occur," Myers says.

Keep calm and stall

Someone is attempting to control you may induce one to reply immediately. When you are angry and fearful, you could devote yourself before fully considering different possibilities.

This is part of why the blackmail functions. Instead, stay as Serene as possible and notify them you will need time.

Try out some variant of, "I cannot decide today. I will consider It and provide you my response afterward."

They could keep forcing you to pick instantly, but Do not back down (or increase to risks). Calmly repeat that you require time.

Begin a conversation

The time you purchase yourself might help you create a plan. Your strategy may be based on the conditions, for example, behavior and the requirement.

"First, check for individual security," Myers urges. "If you feel mentally and physically safe doing this, you can participate in a dialogue."

Most blackmailers know precisely what they're doing. They need their needs fulfilled and do not care about what this costs you.

Others just see their behavior as a strategy that accomplishes their targets and do not understand how it's bothering you. Here, a dialog can greatly increase their consciousness.

"Express the way their words or behaviors cause you to feel," Myers suggests. "Give them a chance to change those behaviors."

Identify your triggers

Someone trying to control you normally has a fairly good Concept of how to push your buttons.

If you dislike arguing in people, as an example, perhaps they threaten to produce a scene.

Based on Myers, increasing your Comprehension of these Fears or beliefs that provide the blackmailer power could offer a chance to take back that power. This can make it considerably harder for another man to use them.

In this Exact Same case, perhaps that means understanding that people Disagreements are a sore spot for you and inventing a normal reaction to this danger.

Enlist them compromise

When you provide another person the Opportunity That Will Help You find an alternate answer, your refusal might seem similar to you.

Begin with a statement that validates their feelings; subsequently open the door to collaborative difficulty.

Perhaps you inform your spouse, "I am hearing you feel mad because I am spending the weekend with my pals. Would you help me understand why you are feeling frustrated?"

This reveals another man you care about how they feel and tells them you are prepared to work together.

Typical Traits of Narcissists and Gaslighters

Gaslighting is a form of manipulation that is constant and Brainwashing that results in the sufferer doubting himself or herself, and to finally lose an individual's own awareness of perception, individuality, and self-worth. A gaslighter's statements and accusations are usually based on willful falsehoods and calculated marginalization. The expression gaslighting comes from the 1944 movie Gaslight, in which a husband attempts to convince his wife that she is mad by inducing her to question herself and her truth.

1. Frequent Lies and Exaggerations

The two narcissists and gaslighters are prone to regular lies and exaggerations (about others and themselves), and have the propensity of lifting up themselves by putting down others. While narcissists often attempt to make themselves look superior and "particular" by displaying, bragging, taking undeserved credit, and other sorts of self-aggrandizement, gaslighters tend to focus on helping you feel poor through false accusations, continuous criticism, and emotional intimidation. The two narcissists and gaslighters may be skillful at distortion of truth, willful falsehoods, character assassinations, and unwanted coercions. 1 key difference is that while the narcissist lies and exaggerates to enhance their delicate self-worth, the gaslighter does to fortify their control and domination.

2. Rarely Admit Flaws and Why Are Aggressive When Criticized

Most narcissists and gaslighters have thin skin and may react badly when called to account for their negative behavior. When contested, the narcissist is very likely to fight (e.g., temper tantrum, excuse-making, denial, blame, hypersensitivity, etc.) or take flight (bolt out of the door, avoidance, quiet treatment, sulking bitterness, or alternative kinds of passive aggression). The gaslighter almost always escalated by doubling or tripling back on their false accusations or coercion, to bully or oppress their own opponent. Many gaslighters see relationships as inherently aggressive instead of collaborative; a zero-sum match at which one is a winner or a loser, either at the top or in the base. "Crime is the best defense" is a mantra for several gaslighters, signifying their competitive way of relating to individuals.

3. False Image Projection

"My husband always needs people to view him successful, Strong, and envy-worthy, however shaky his actual life really is." --Anonymous spouse of narcissist

The two narcissists and gaslighters are inclined to project untrue, Idealized pictures of these into the planet, so as to conceal their internal workings. Many narcissists prefer to impress others by making themselves seem great. This "decoration complicated" can display itself , romantically, physically, socially, religiously, financially, materially, professionally, academically, or culturally. The underlying message of the screen is:"I am much better than you!" Or "Look at just how particular I'm -- I am worthy of everybody's love, respect, and approval!"

On the other hand, gaslighters frequently create an idealized Self-image of being the most dominant, suppressive alpha female or male in private relationships, in the office, or at high profile places of society (for instance, politics and media). Many gaslighters prefer to see themselves as all-powerful and powerful, capable of dishing out penalties and decisions whatsoever. Pathological gaslighters frequently take pride and encourage them by marginalizing those they perceive as weaker, presuming the meek deserve their downtrodden fate. They assault their victims with subtle or direct cruelty and contempt, gaining malevolent pleasure from these types of crimes, and betraying a lack of compassion and humanity.

Essentially, narcissists need others to worship them, while Gaslighters want other people to submit to them. Hugely, these outside facades become critical portions of their false identities, substituting the insecure and real ego.

4. Rule Breaking and Boundary Violation

Most narcissists and gaslighters love getting away with Violating rules and societal norms. Cases of narcissistic trespass contain cutting line, chronic under-tipping, private space intrusion, borrowing things without returning, other's possessions without inquiring, disobeying traffic laws, busting appointments, etc negating promises. Cases of gaslighting trespass include subtle or direct marginalizing opinions, private or public shaming and humiliation, sardonic humor and amusing remarks, net trolling, mad and hateful speech, and virulent attacks on undesirable people and groups.

The two narcissist and gaslighter border offenses presume Entitlement, using a narrow, egocentric orientation that oppresses and de-humanizes their sufferers. In acute cases, this border violation pathology might come in illegal and underhanded dealings, financial abuse, physical harassment, date rape, domestic abuse, hate crimes, human rights violations, and other criminality types. Most narcissists and gaslighters enjoy their own harmful behaviors, as their machinations supply them with a hollow (and desperate) feeling of superiority and freedom.

5. Emotional Invalidation and Coercion

Even though narcissists and gaslighters could be (but aren't constantly) physically abusive, for the vast majority of their victims, psychological suffering is the point where the harm is painfully felt. The two narcissists and gaslighters enjoy dispersing and stimulating negative emotions to feel strong and help you stay insecure and insecure. They routinely invalidate others' ideas, emotions, and disposition, demonstrating little remorse for inducing individuals in their own lives pain. They frequently blame their victims for getting their own victimization ("You would not get yelled at in the event that you were not so dumb!") .

Additionally, many narcissists and gaslighters possess erratic mood swings and have a tendency toward psychological play -- you will never know what may displease them and put them off. They get mad at any indicators of liberty and self-affirmation ("Who do you believe you're!?") . They flip agitated if you disagree with their views or don't satisfy their expectations. As stated before, they're sensitive to criticism, but fast to judge others. By keeping you down and allow you to feel poor, they improve their delicate self, and feel reassured about them.

6. Manipulation: The Control or Use Others as an Extension of Oneself

The two narcissists and gaslighters have a Propensity to create Choices for other people to suit their particular schedule. Narcissists can use their intimate spouse, child, family, friend, or colleague to satisfy unreasonable self-serving wants, fulfill unrealized fantasies, or cover up flaws and shortcomings. Narcissists are also fond of using blame, guilt, and victimhood as manipulative devices.

Gaslighters conduct emotional manipulation toward Groups and individuals through persistent stimulation of the fact, to cause their victims to question themselves and feel confident. In professional or personal surroundings, they control by micromanaging (controlling) connections, such as telling others how they ought to think, feel, and act beneath the gaslighter's unreasonable restrictions and evaluation. They frequently become very critical, angry, frightening, or aggressive toward those who don't bow down to their own directives. Gaslighter manipulation is frequently highly competitive, together with punitive measures (real or emotional) implemented toward individuals who don't comprehend and comply with their own self-perceived authority.

Perhaps the biggest distinction between narcissists and Gaslighters is that narcissists utilize and harness, and gaslighters control and dominate. Though the narcissist does to compensate for a dire sense of lack (of being unloved as the actual self), the gaslighter does to conceal their ever-present insecurity (of being helpless and losing management). Both these behavioral forms betray a inability or unwillingness to connect with individuals genuinely and equitably as individual beings.

They eventually become "particular" and "exceptional" by being human and from de-humanizing others.

From the worst-case scenario, some people have traits of the two narcissism and gaslighting. This is an extremely poisonous and damaging blend of abuse, vanity, bullying, and misuse -- all unleashed as a way to compensate for the perpetrator's deep-seated awareness of inadequacy and anxiety.

Hoovering and the Narcissistic Victim

The expression hoovering derives in the vacuum cleaner Company, Hoover, and invokes the organization's vacuum cleaner' method of sucking items in, just like the narcissistic abuser sucks back the victim to the emotionally and, paradoxically, physically abusive relationship.

Throughout the process, the narcissist abuser may use any way necessary to receive their desired outcome: the sufferer's yield into the abusive relationship. These ploys may include things like trying to set the victim on a guilt-trip, creating false claims of altered behavior, false claims of too-good-to-be-true presents, begging, yelling at the sufferer, usage of connection shame, which makes risks, insincerely accepting blame for the collapse of their connection, or even with other people (flying monkeys) to help convince the victim to go back to the relationship. The abusive narcissist is really on a no-holds-barred effort to convince the victim to come back to the abuse along with their abusive clutches.

Regrettably, these abusive narcissists triumph in their efforts. This has been evidenced to me in the street level for a police officer when I'd be called back into the scene of a domestic dispute or domestic violence telephone where I was formerly.

How can this occur? Why would somebody knowingly return to a violent relationship?

There is a procedure, near the Exact Same procedure the abusive Narcissist employed from the connection previously.

Step One

They're kind, loving, and compassionate. They'll say fine Things they think the victim would like to hear. They'll try to court the sufferer and woo them with their fake charm. But if this doesn't work, they might proceed into another stage.

Step Two

They are verbally abusive and try to convince the Prey that nobody else will need them, they are damaged, not quite enough, not smart enough, or not worthy of anybody else. Their degradation might be infinite. The sufferer may also hear the abusive narcissist only desires what's ideal for the victim or is looking for the sufferer. If this measure doesn't succeed in compelling the victim to reunite, step three could then be utilized.

Step Three

That really is their Hail Mary pass. This is where the violent Narcissist tries to destroy what the sufferer holds dear to themselves. This may come as strikes on their intellect, abilities as parents, job skills or standing, business positions, or another item the victim holds precious. Not unusual is their endeavor to convince the sufferer which, not only does the narcissist think they're a failure at any one of these things but "everybody else" also considers the same. This process Can Begin at any time, immediately following the Break-up as well as many decades after.

What are a few of the Specific ploys the abusive narcissist may Use to acquire the sufferer's control and get her to reunite?

The narcissist's creativity just constrains the ploys. A number of those ploys may comprise:

1. Sending the unexpected sufferer messages stating how much they overlook the sufferer or that they adore the abused person.
2. Contacting the sufferer on purposeful dates like prior birthdays, anniversaries, or new landmarks in the sufferer's life.
3. Asking for assistance. This might include things like having your urgent help in their house or requesting assistance in a medical situation or psychological stress condition. Maybe they might say they are just about to commit suicide to receive a response from the sufferer. This is only one of the more important signals of hoovering using a narcissist.
4. Sending Presents for no reason. The abusive narcissist could send flowers, cards, or other presents as a means to reach out and tug in the sufferer's heartstrings.
5. Promising Luxurious presents such as holidays, a new auto, even a new residence.
6. Acting as Though the preceding abuse never occurred and try to restart a dialogue with the victim.
7. Pleading and begging for just one more opportunity to make it all right.

8. Saying they're so, so in love. The sufferer could hear the way the abuser wants to express his undying love and assure the loving relationship the sufferer has ever desired.

Listed below are just offender reasons a narcissist participates in hovering:

1. A narcissist returns since, in their thoughts, they Perceive people as things and in this instance possessions.

To a narcissist, a spouse is only victim, an item serving their pleasure. From this view of human relationships, a narcissist regards failure for a hazard. He ****, it is inconceivable to eliminate control of a person they intentionally trapped together with the entire assortment of real-life abuse tactics. He is back to prove who is "exceptional" and who is "poor" by devoting ownership. He returns to show he's controlling, as an instance, the capability to destabilize a person's lifetime, to con and love-bomb them lies into thinking more fairy tale illusions, once more, merely to allow them to exploit and utilize them such as punching bags, etc.

In the brain of a narcissist, a ownership is obviously a possession. Leaving is never an alternative. Things do not leave; they do not possess a Head of their own. They serve the whims of owners. In the instance of cancerous

Narcissists (APDs), this explains why leaving them demanding they leave, is If they post the best threat and risk to other people.

2. A narcissist is an enthusiast, and so constantly preoccupied Using their next fix.

A narcissist views others as items to exploit for personal gain. He also hoovers to reengage a trustworthy drug source, heartlessly re-opening a previous spouse's old wounds to"re-enable" that the supply. To him prior partner is not anything more than a place to find a "repair," and they reunite when conducting low in receiving repairs, or at times of scarcity but also, like a juggler, to maintain an supply-source rotation and accessible. Now you could say, why would a person do this? Do not they have a life?Based onto a narcissist's thought-disordered worldview, with other people to have a repair is it, what lifestyle and enjoyment is about.

Every repair, into a narcissist, is a success, one which adds to His false-self sense of excellence. And that's his cure, period. When he behaves and states loving and caring things, it's not loving, it's love-bombing, a strategy used as part of their bigger plan, in this circumstance, to disarm and lure the "individual" forms they prey and look down with scorn, so as to gain their confidence. Bear in mind, they research and understand their prey, mainly girls. When they love-bomb they intentionally speak in a way that make girls swoon -- using an ulterior motive to exploit them. He says and does functions to find another fix, and the following.

3. A narcissist's medication of choice relies on violating the rights of others.

Narcissists are chronic abusers. At minimum, psychological and Psychological. Like addicts, they intentionally attempt to inflict pain or violate their spouse's rights. From that disordered mindset, if a individual could be tricked and receive "hurt," which makes them dumb and weak -- and also the narcissist powerful and smart. Violating other people with no guilt is related to a rigid belief system which, in varying amounts from boyhood, shames guys to exhibit a callous disregard to their spouse's feelings to prove they deserve the status of belonging to the "cult of masculinity."

To them, strength and excellence have been shown on the basis of How heartlessly you can re-capture, fool and subvert the will and head of an older partner, by way of instance, to increase their hopes only to dash them to throw them off course, to establish who is still got the best dog standing by, once more, tearing down a previous spouse's awareness of self, value, and instill them with pity, uncertainty, fear, confusion, and of course rejection, jealousy, worthlessness, and so on. Domestic violence, physical assault, rape, pedophilia, mass shootings have something in common: they're patterns of behavior exhibited by (mostly) guys that identify and operate 24/7 to apply the principles for "poisonous masculinity.")

4. A narcissist yields to prove (what he perceives As)"entitlements" to abuse and exploit with impunity.

To a narcissist, a previous partner is a physical thing he is willing to exploit indefinitely. He proceeds to prove he is still has the ability to mistreat her because he wants, and in return hopes she treats him infallible and entitled. And, he's constantly on guard to protect and keep up a double standard in regards to entitlements. Gaslighting is his favorite instrument to derail the attention of any dialog to serve his objectives. He gaslights, and relishes the power that this gives him (supplying she remains unaware of her reality and his lies) to turn every conversation into a nightmare, and also to state her step by step to silence himself, never to bring her up pain, desires, demands, and also to blame herself for his distress.

According to his belief in male dominance and superiority, he Feels entitled to hoard the advantages and delights from the relationship. It's a con game, also in this circumstance, the artwork of erecting illusions and implanting false-self pictures of these as with godlike powers, even while ripping their victim's feeling of self and service, relies on clinically recognized techniques of thought-control. All cult leaders from the way, spiritual and secular, are malignant narcissists, fulfilling the standards for narcissism about the intense array of narcissism, which is antisocial personality disorder (APD), also called psychopathology. Meanwhile certain romanticized fantasies women are conditioned to think from youth make them easy prey for narcissists.

5. A narcissist returns to maintain a previous partner trapped in an emotional roller coaster, manipulated by lies and illusions, captured in exactly the very same patterns of hope-then-let down and powerlessness.

A narcissist could only be known in their worldview, None! He's proud to be called ruthless, callous toward women's annoyance, a ferocious rival vying to hold on every piece of their energy in a connection, and to leave his spouse helpless. (A covert narcissist does so in hidden ways, painting himself as a pleasant, laid back man, commanded and emasculated by his spouse.) He lusts to hate and be hated, so he is happy to no end if he will get his partner to say that she hates him and behaves violently toward him. (Unlike him, she'll probably feel bad then; this provides him dual enjoyment, also makes it simpler to fault and blame her.) Hence he works to make her feel every bit as gloomy, self-loathing, scheming, vying for power, callous, unfeeling, detached, etc, as he is. He works hard to create her fear and despise him.

Though he would deny it, he worries feelings of vulnerability as Indications of flaws and inferiority, and works hard to deny, reject, and suppress them and other men. These feelings include his true self; at least once he had been born. His upbringing he to fear and refuse his true self! It means that his false self doesn't exist! He has been shamed from boyhood, conditioned to instruct him to deny and disown some of the feelings of tenderness -- which would stop him from showing "actual" man feelings like no guilt and callousness toward a female's pain!

6. A narcissist returns to the sadistic pleasure of damaging the individual who tried to adore him.

A narcissist is addicted to deriving pleasure from damaging others, which makes them feel awful, increasing expectations to dash hopes. Call it what it is, real life abuse! This kind of abuse contains deliberate acts of injury. To the level, it triggers a group of symptoms, much like PTSD on the 1 hand, and Stockholm Syndrome on another, and a disease, not yet recorded in the DSM refer to as: hemorrhagic abuse syndrome. By simply holding fast to the distressed mindset, narcissists condemn themselves to endure a lifetime of misery and self-loathing; and because misery loves company, that signifies a lifetime of working hard to make others feel as though they feel indoors: gloomy, lonely, delicate, protected, disillusioned, confused, trapped, helpless, etc..

Making those they deem week squirm to, spin their Wheels, etc., and is a drug that offers relief -- their very best buddy, like a jar of whiskey is to an alcoholic. Their drug of choice numbs the pain and distress inside, and such as addicts, they vehemently deny any responsibility due to their distress. They're hooked on deriving pleasure from making others feel unhappy. A miserable bunch, they think that this proves their excellence. (This explains the fact that truth is their main enemy, and they dread nothing more than fact and truth-tellers.)

7. A narcissist contributes to fortify the lies that he needs his Prey to trust about him and self, others and life.

In a narcissists perspective, people exist in dichotomous and Adversarial classes of superior versus poor, strong versus weak, meant-to-rule versus meant-to-be-ruled, male versus female, white versus nonwhite, and thus on. Thus, narcissists come back to fortify the illusions and dreams they invent to perform god. They're busy illusionists, on 24/7 so to speak, strategizing to change and remain in control of the way others to believe, what they think, the way the universe of connections operate, etc.. The narcissist lies on matters, large and small. In comparison To "routine" lies that are protective or defensive, most of the lies of a narcissist are offensive in character. They lie to promote a worldview where their "false-self" excellence is actual, a belief that jelqing violence and cruelty as way for "powerful" men to keep dominance within the "feeble" This clarifies why a narcissist won't modify! To change is not to exist. To these, "recovery" speaks solely the weak participate in. Really, their biggest fear is that the true self of others and self -- human being! They desperately attempt to refuse or pathologies individual yearnings for intimacy, closeness, and collaboration. They want lies since their false self doesn't exist within a world of facts about the energy of love and imagination, cooperation and individual relationship!

In summary, previous spouses beware! A narcissist does not respect a previous partner as an individual being. Really, he believes scorn for individual traits and ideals. The individuality of a narcissist is wed to acts of others, and in the process, making they look like the "ordinary" ones, even while smearing their critics or victims to make them seem emotionally crazy or bad.

The belief system that he retains drives his activities and the Pathological patterns of behavior, the underlying notions and bodily feeling conditions. Identify and get to understand the traps they set, the lure they throw, and then avoid these like the plague.

What do you have to cure and put yourself free?

For someplace where your main Aim is to love and honor and respect life and yourself, your greatest goals is to allow the narcissist go, refuse to provide them some area in your heart, soul and mind except to thank the Universe for learning in the experience to better appreciate and accept yourself and lifestyle!

Kinds of lure narcissists use to control & manipulate - And what you could do about it.

In learning how to handle this and moving from Narcissistic abuse, it can be quite beneficial in the first case to learn how to recognize any lure only for what it is

- an effort to catch your attention and pull you in. The next step is to learn how to recognize the variety of lure and then function to resist the desire to bite! Awareness of what a narcissist is performing, jointly with self-awareness of how this leaves you sense can truly help with this.

Basically, we could group the various Kinds of narcissistic Lure under two chief classes - fear & guilt and anxiety & obligation.

Whatever the Particular lure is and yet blatant or subtle, it'll be utilized with the purpose of attempting to activate at least one of the aforementioned feelings in you. That's because if we're anxious, fearful, feeling remorse or too accountable, we are a lot simpler to manipulate.

Recognizing the lure for what it's can take the energy from its own effect.

Some common examples of lure comprise:

Fear-provoking & scaremongering - these comprise any tries to elicit fear and nervousness in you or other people. A narcissist will appear to essentially attune to your precise fears, anxieties or insecurities.

Intrigue - classic interracial fishing method of attempting to pull in. Normally a snippet of vague or info, intrigue-inducing remark is supplied so as to activate the ofter persons fear or intrigue. They might or might not elaborate further - hence aiming to excite more stress or intrigue. With this, they've captured you and your focus.

False accusations - This Kind of lure is one that can frequently Trip up people and keep them secured into an unhealthy energetic. Like every type of lure, together with false accusations, the narcissist is searching for a response. They might or might not even feel the accusation they could cause you personally, but with this lure they are working to rely on our instinctive propensity to protect ourselves, to deny, justify or correct some incorrect views others might have around us. (A narcissist will consider what they want to no matter so that you may as well just leave them!)

Guilt-tripping - feelings of guilt may go hand-in-hand with then feeling too responsible. Guilt and anxiety are just two things that may make a meltdown in our bounds - that is exactly what the narcissist is finally and generally hoping to achieve when they're trying to guilt-trip.

Victim - another kind of manipulative bait would be to portray themselves as the 'poor me' victim. With this lure they are working to evoke your sympathy, compassion and understanding and also avoid taking responsibility. They plan to reel others to some care-taking, adjusting or rescuing position.

False-hope - this really is actually the hanging of the carrot on a series especially in what they know is important for you or whatever you need in life. The dream idea is introduced that they'll give you with this but it's only used as lure to allow you to stay or to command in any other manner.

The Way to handle the lure
To start with it is important to learn how to recognize the lure.
Which are the different kinds of lure you recognize with the entire Narcissist in your mind? Be as specific as you can.
Are there certain forms that especially affect you or create Holding boundaries hard? How can such lure make you feel? Then what exactly do you do?

A strong shift can happen when you begin to reevaluate the Lure for exactly what it is... an effort to reel you in, grab and control.

You Might Even Have the Ability to Start to forecast another bait tactic.

Do not take anything the narcissist says or does. Attempt to leave them.

Recognize lure as a lure and more importantly, notice how that leaves you feeling. Notice the instant impulse in you as to how you might want or feel the necessity to respond.

Bear in Mind, for any narcissist, Any Sort of reaction that they can Illegal in other people is a twisted manner in which they attempt to feel better about themselves.

Whilst you (or anyone else) are responding strongly to them, you're reinforcing the message they have control and power.

You can Learn How to handle your responses by getting more mindfully aware of these. You don't have to demonstrate that the narcissist your response.

You can also Learn How to stop biting the bait once you concentrate more on recognizing your feelings and then attending that along with your needs appropriately.

The Way to Establish Boundaries With A Narcissist: Is There A Way To Do That?

Lacking compassion for the way their actions affect other people, Narcissists feel entitled to utilize different men and women. This makes it particularly important to establish firm boundaries together. Here are seven powerful approaches:

1. Do not justify, explain, or defend yourself. Narcissists Utilize evaluation or intimidation to create others. Doing this gives them a sense of control and power.

Section of boundary-setting is your best to decide what you share with other people. The less you discuss, especially private information, the a narcissist must use.

You do not have to justify your ideas, feelings, or Activities into a intrusive narcissist. When a narcissist criticizes you, then it is possible to say something like, "I hear that your view and I shall think about that." Should they question your activities, state, "I'm confident in my selection." Should they need an excuse, say, "That's private," or "We will need to just agree to disagree"

2. Leave when it does not feel healthier. You do not need Anybody's consent to depart a damaging interaction. You, others, get to ascertain what's healthy for you.

You are able to glance at your watch and say, "Look at the time: I am late." Then leave. Late for what? It does not matter. Every time you stay in the existence of violent or controlling behavior makes you late for healthy self-care. Your phone may be helpful prop. Nobody can understand for sure if you have received a telephone. Say, "I am sorry, I must take this call" Then leave. Or pick in advance how many minutes you wish to provide a narcissist, then place your telephone or watch alarm to go off in the moment. After the alarm sounds, excuse you. Or directly face unhealthy therapy by stating something Enjoy, "I will excuse myself. We can speak another time when you're prepared for a constructive dialog," or, "This really isn't healthy. I won't take part in this type of conversation"

3. Choose what you will endure and what you want. A key part of establishing healthy boundaries is knowing when to say no, and doing this. Ask yourself exactly what you are prepared to take from the others and what you aren't. By way of instance, you might be fine with good-natured banter although not sarcasm. You might be OK with enthusiastic expressions of opinions but not name-calling or bullying.

1 method of drawing the line would be to state, "Should you continue to call me names, I'll finish our conversation till you're inclined to treat me with respect" You do not have to clarify further. When a narcissist's aggressive behavior continues, leave or hang out. Refuse to take part in additional discussion, regardless of what they say or do.

When you place such bounds, narcissists may cycle through their repertoire: contending; blaming; decreasing your feelings; behaving like a victim; stating that you are overly sensitive; or getting rageful. While these approaches can be disagreeable to survive, your boundaries aren't up for debate.

4. Learn to sidestep intrusive queries or Negative remarks. Skilled governmental spin doctors resisted difficult questions from journalists simply by answering another question -- normally, a question they wanted they were requested to encourage their own agenda.

Likewise if a narcissist inquires an intrusive question, you can change topics. If a narcissist that has a history of criticizing your spending, career options, or individual relationships starts their recognizable interrogation, why measure in that? Instead, say something like, "These are the sorts of challenges which build character, are not they?"

Or change to some subject the narcissist loves to discuss. Request their perspectives on the key to a fantastic connection or the way they made a challenging profession or fiscal option.

While their replies may be filled with platitudes, at least they will concentrate on their favorite subject -- themselves -- rather than you. You might even pick up a few thoughts. Additionally, it may feel advocating to adeptly changing a dialogue.

5. Pick out the bully by the horns. Narcissists thirst for Focus and acceptance to counteract profound, unconscious feelings of bitterness and unworthiness. Because of this, they endlessly examine to learn what they can get away with.

1 way to satisfy this would be to call out what they're doing. For Example, say, "Are you really attempting to put me down or cause me to feel awful?" Or, "I notice that if I start to speak, you interrupt me"

Matter-of-factly say these matters. It does not matter how they react. Be cautious in knowing you've named what's occurring, and leave it at that.

6. Do not underestimate the power of narcissism. Recall that narcissists have spent a lifetime learning the way to digitize and make the most of the others. Narcissism is a potent psychological phenomenon based on twisted perspectives of self, others, and the planet.

The majority of individuals are unnerved by narcissistic strategies. And should you Come out of a narcissistic upbringing or have a long-term relationship with a narcissist, you might be prepared to take unhealthy behavior.

If you do not establish healthy boundaries in a given situation, have compassion on your own. Identify exactly what you would like to do differently next time and proceed. Boundary-setting isn't a one-time occasion.

7. Recall: Great boundaries contain impacts. Section of placing Boundaries understands what you're ready to do in case your borders are ignored. Consequences are greatest when they're clear in your mind beforehand. Afterward, when a border is broken, behave on your preferred consequence instantly, decisively, each and every moment. Otherwise, you might get rid of credibility.

Insidious Ways Narcissistic Abuse Isolates that the Victim
It looks like everyone is speaking about narcissism those days. Do social media strain it? Are we raising a

generation of overpraised narcissistic children? Is the boss, your new flirtation, or even your president ? Questions and concepts abound. But suppose you are dealing with the nightmare of someone near you with narcissistic character disorder. In that case, you will need help knowing how earnest misuse isolates individuals and everything to do about it.

How Narcissistic Abuse Isolates

Narcissists possess an arsenal of abuses; however, solitude is just one Of the foremost weapons. Isolating targeted victims empowers the narcissist to manipulate and control them. If it comes to their spouse and kids, they isolate them in the external world, from one another, and also by their own sense of reality. To make things worse, hardly any individuals really understand narcissism, isolating victims even further.

1. Narcissistic Abuse Isolates You against the External World

Seeking continuously (like in each hour of each day) to Convince others, and possibly more themselves, their false mask of excellence is actual, narcissists isolate those near to them to restrain everything "their loved ones" reflect and show about them. The narcissist generally most isolates family members since they pose the largest threat of showing things about her/himself which s/he doesn't want known. S/he keeps careful watch over what household info and graphics are vulnerable to the external world.

2. Narcissistic Abuse Isolates You from Family Members

Another go-to approach of this narcissist is to split and conquer. Within households, narcissists ruthlessly put members against the other. 1 method they use is to deal with kids inequitably, favoring targeting and one other. Narcissists also make a competitive and threatening setting that keeps relatives vying for acceptance or a reprieve from assault. Attack can take several forms, such as anger, ridicule, as well as attribute. Narcissists isolate their spouse with risks, interrogation, belittlement, and violent outbursts. The spouse may permit the narcissist's isolating approaches by encouraging branches within the household.

3. Narcissistic Abuse Isolates You Yourself

The Greatest puppeteer, the narcissist frequently gaslights (leads other people to question their judgment and sanity) relatives, denies their truth, and endeavors her/his own misuse and tainted agenda on them. The narcissist always generates the experience of cognitive dissonance in the others--a battle between what you feel/see to become authentic and that which s/he tells you is occurring. Cognitive dissonance interrupts the inherent link between your emotions and your awareness of fact, in nature separating you out of you--drilling a schism via your heart, where you come to essentially doubt yourself.

4. Narcissistic Abuse Isn't Understood

Jazz great Louis Armstrong famously stated, "There is some People, that, if they do not understand, you cannot teller" A lot of men and women lack the creativity to comprehend matters beyond their immediate experience. However, to add insult to dreadful harm, narcissistic personality disorder is indeed especially complicated, laborious, callous, and damaging it is practically impossible to understand unless you have lived it (or anything like this) firsthand. Even if they understand something about the disease, most of us don't know what narcissistic abuse actually involves, and they're unaware of its own deep and lasting psychological and bodily injury.

Even survivors themselves, once from the narcissist, Struggle, comprehend what they were through and heal from it. But if survivors reach out for assistance, their relatives, friends, pastors, as well as therapists may neglect to recognize the abuse and ignore their expertise, further endangering them.

Chapter 3 Traits Narcissists Search For Their Victims

Trait Number One: Unhealed Traumas

The amount one worldwide strategy to get a narcissist to enmesh With a different, including a love or business partner, friend, neighbor or perhaps in respect to some household of source narcissist hoping to keep another relative for distribution -- is that:

Locate the 'need' and indicate to be the expansive provider of it.

Narcissists question possible romantic partner targets to learn what still damaging them is missing in respect to their past love life.

If you state that you're treated as you did not matter, the Narcissist will provide the information to allow you to think that to him or her you may completely matter. If your prior traumas have been around adultery, then the narcissist will likely be 100% monogamous.

In a business context, the narcissist will supposedly have the smarts, experience, contacts, and confidence you don't have.

When a Relative is ready to pull off and walk off, that the narcissist may feign to function as caring, considerate person that another family member has all their lifetime.

Suppose you are feeling empty, frustrated, helpless or ineffectual in some area of your life. In that case, you're vulnerable to being scammed and mistreated by a narcissist faking to be the savior of the injury.

Obviously, Most of Us have things that people need, yet if we're not accepting personal responsibility to cure those feelings in ourselves, we'll be destitute. We'll catch an external solution instead of doing the internal work to develop into a psychological recovery alternative to ourselves.

This means we could make risky decisions, rather than simply take our Time to determine individuals' character and be certain that our bounds, body, heart, thoughts and house have been allowed the healthier due diligence to keep them secure.

After we are complete, we do not hurry things. When we are vacant and destitute we become irresponsible to attempt and find relief from our internal insecurities and anxieties about the future.

Trait Number 2: Not Honouring Your Inner Being

Narcissists understand how to examine people's boundaries. When narcissists goals you as a possible source, they're looking for out whether you honor yourself, your worth and your precision.

Because If You is in your power, once the narcissist Starts breaking up your bounds and mining you using their very own self-serving agendas, you may put a stop to your relationship.

Someone tasked with living their truths and values will not be a game for these behaviors.

Narcissists can quickly test your borders, particularly if He or she's managed to hook up fast along with you, and infiltrate your own time, Emotions and lifestyle. Now, you may already be feeling a psychological Dependence on this individual as the supplier of this love, acceptance, safety or Survival you haven't yet solved within yourself.

You Might Even Begin experiencing disgusting offenses of your Rights and values which begin ripping your soul apart. Sooner or later in your relationship with the narcissist, these horrible experiences are unavoidable.

If You Begin acquiescing to Attempt to maintain the peace, or perhaps Fight back since it has hurt you personally, instead of make supreme boundaries, pull out and understand what you will or won't have on your own life -- that the narcissist will now understand he or she is able to violate you mine you and comprehend exactly what he or she would like.

Identically, upon fulfilling a narcissist, he or she's manners of analyzing your boundaries and visiting if you're likely to perform your due diligence and take your own time to estimate her or his private character or not.

Should you begin mechanically anticipating and gravitating towards a narcissist, regardless of the warning signals your Inner Being is completely supplying you (this happened to us), then the narcissist has a green light to move.

Trait Number Three: Not Getting Your Own Whole Life

1 part of becoming that injured gazelle in the edge of this Pack, capable of being chosen with a predator, isn't having a complete, happy and productive life

You see, This Is the Way it goes narcissists Will Need to make dependencies.

If you feel lonely, empty and have just been going through The moves waiting for something to change out yourself, or to get someone to turn up so as to begin giving you a happy productive life, you're in danger. That somebody who you need to be the savior of the emptiness is somebody who you will fight greatly to let go of -- regardless of how badly he or she treats you.

If, when you begin connecting with someone in a healthy Speed, you do not sustain your personal life, joy, and purpose then that individual becomes your 'everything'.

That is dire; it's unhealthy co-dependent attachment. It Means this individual's decisions, life and values will become your personal, however violent and disordered they could be.

Additionally, it means that this Individual can monopolies your emotions, Life and time speedily.

In stark comparison, keeping yourself, your life and your Worth is one of the most significant defenses in respect to not being accepted down and in with a narcissist. They aren't going to endure it and will have to depart from your experience.

Trait Number Four: Being Able to Lose Everything to Get It All

If You Aren't prepared to enjoy yourself first and foremost, then you're vulnerable to being mistreated by someone who you're working to receive your own sense of value and enjoy from.

A Wholesome lifestyle in regard to social relationships needs to Begin with self-love. If a person begins treating you in violent and unhealthy ways that you love yourself enough to pull off and align with the self indulgent, 'I love myself enough to learn more suffer abuse'.

Normally, narcissists do something improper, uncaring Or even violent early in the connection. Or maybe you discover questionable or information actions concerning this individual who simply don't add up, or point-blank expose her or him to be no wonderful person.

If you create excuses to Remain connected, and if You're not ready to pull off and make security around the sanctity of your spirit and life-force by announcing the facts of your worth and what you will and will not accept in life, the narcissist knows he or she is able to be a creature and you won't leave.

The narcissist knows You'll remain attached Attempting to alter Them so as to attempt to get a joyful life. This gives the narcissist with copious quantities of real time supply -- the play and care that he or she receives from understanding how badly this influence you. He or she now has you as a goal to beat to offload their internal demons onto.

If you are someone who is willing to shed it all to do it all, meaning shed another individual instead of lose yourself, you'll never be vulnerable to your narcissist. You'll leave when things begin to feel and turn into 'away'. You may set the limits about what you will and will not accept, and you'll very quickly understand that the narcissist doesn't have the tools to really meet you.

Suppose you're currently curing to get to this newfound Actual Self Power. In that case, you may eventually escape the clutches of narcissistic abuse and begin to split out the life that's reflective of your Authentic Self.

Obviously, to be strong enough on the inside to perform this requires doing the internal work on your initial traumas so as to become complete. Otherwise, you might capitulate and maintain handing away your power.

Trait Number Five: Attempting to Change Others to Stop Them from Hurting You

Narcissists seek out co-dependent individuals. All these are individuals who make other people company their company to attempt and feel loved, happy, and safe.

They are often edgy, reckless, live high on the hog, and show little respect for principles, responsibility and finances. After all it's all about feeding their insatiable False self to be able to feel important, irrespective of the price.

Suppose You're Somebody Who is covertly controlling, meaning Accepting responsibility for other men and women who do not take responsibility for themselves, so that one to feel secure on the interior. In that case, you're an ideal fit for a narcissist.

He or she needs someone to wash up the messes. He or she needs anybody to keep the flames burning while the narcissist pursues fresh supply outside the house. He or she needs someone to hang about and remain centered on the narcissist no matter how poorly the narcissist acts.

We might believe It Is caring to care for reckless And out-of-control men and women, but actually this is an effort to attempt and have individuals to be secure and secure so they can appreciate us and care for us.

As kids, we might have been linked to dangerous others, attempting to resolve things for them that they would be secure. The truth is that we had no other alternative. As adults we all do, and we could not mend other people's behavior to receive our own supply of love, acceptance, survival and security.

We only ever attain these items by letting go of Individuals Who we think need fixing turning inwards and adjusting the actual reasons why we've inclined to do so and remain connected to mistreat in debilitating relationships.

Trait Number Six: You Aren't Self-Partnered and Loving Yourself

After the narcissist begins behaving in inappropriate and Abusive manners, and you remain connected to him or her rather than pulling off to care for yourself, the narcissist knows he or she has been the center of the world.

The narcissist will keep hurting you, taking and mining from you, and understanding you have been procured as a distribution source while this occurs.

When you remain, so tolerating things which you never thought you'd endure, the narcissist has full permission to relax and shed the mask even further.

They may realize that if caught out with adultery You will not leave.

This can be soul-destroying for you, when you realize your the main point is virtually completely extinguished, or non-existent today.

This Is why being self-partnered is your amount 1 step to consider, to begin pulling away, recovering, bringing yourself back into wholeness and health and being impervious to abusers later on.

It's the complete basis of recovery from the Thriver Way to be able to make a complete recovery of not only your misuse symptoms, but also your misuse patterns.

Suppose You Aren't self-partnered, meaning you are dedicated to Loving yourself enough to cure and make yourself as a healthy and whole person who's no more prone to misuse. In that case, your life is going to probably be ordered by other people's values and decisions instead of your own.

Narcissists Understand How to look out for it to determine in which Folks are in regards to becoming anchored in their being self-love to themselves or never. Individuals who've been delegating different people as their source of love, acceptance, survival and security are definitely not self-partnered.

If this is True, narcissists understand They Can easily Slot within that place, enmesh with individuals, and begin taking over their spirit and life.

The Way to Recuperate From All These Six Traits

I hope that moving over these high six traits that narcissists Watch out for their sufferers has helped you know precisely how you might have been vulnerable to real life abuse.

Many Individuals are extremely conscious of the symptoms they Are suffering. They have been mistreated, but don't realize the actual rectifications that are essential to graduate from their pain and injury to evolve yourself outside handing away your power to abusers back again. If you want additional clarification and understanding about Precisely how this has played out on life then I ask that you join me within my free webinar at which you will begin to know just how you are able to cure from not only your misuse symptoms, but in addition the abuser's ability to hurt you personally, also, going forward, the anxieties of becoming involved in any narcissistic folks later on.

Qualities Malignant Narcissists Search For Their Victims -- And How They Use Them against You

Being mistreated by a narcissist is never a victim's error, in any shape, manner, or form. Everyone can be a target for a psychological predator -- only being human leaves you vulnerable to those poisonous types. That having been said, it's very important to acknowledge the characteristics a narcissist looks for at a goal so that sufferers can protect themselves and reduce ties before on, particularly when they know they're being manipulated.

A Number of These traits are absolutely amazing when they're allowed to flourish in the context of a healthy connection (and if moderated by proper self-care), but using a malignant narcissist they could and will be used against you personally.

1. Conscientiousness.

Perhaps among the most overlooked attributes narcissists Start looking for is your ability to become conscientious. Conscientious people are worried about the others' well-being and follow through on their responsibilities to other people. Because they make conclusions based on their own conscience, they're very likely to project their own sense of morality on the narcissist and suppose that the narcissist also will follow. Narcissists understand that if sufferers are conscientious sufficient to fret about the demands of the others, they could exploit that caliber to serve them.

Malignant predators know that a conscientious man will provide them the benefit of the doubt, will consider in awarding them second chances, and will take care of serving the narcissist's requirements even at the cost of their own. Narcissists understand that because of their aims, this kind of caretaking is linked to the "responsibility" setup from the amorous relationship -- they hope that exceptionally conscientious men and women wish to meet this responsibility, even though it puts them into harm's way.

"Disturbed personalities most often target people possessing two Qualities that they do not contain: conscientiousness and excess agreeableness (i.e. deference). Thus, it is a good conscience that makes you vulnerable to real-life manipulation. Manipulators use shame and guilt because their prime weapons. However, you must possess the capacity for guilt and shame for those approaches to do the job. Disturbed personalities lack that capability. Conscientious people have it in spades." Dr. George Simon, Personalities Prone into Narcissistic Manipulation

2. Empathy.

The significance of owning an empathic target can't be underestimated. Narcissists don't get a excellent steady supply of supply (compliments, care, tools, etc.) from anybody who lacks compassion. They lack compassion, but their preferred targets frequently have a lot of empathy. The psychological fuel that empathic people give the narcissist is crucial for them to sense in power and in control; differently, they basically "starve" and go to the search for a different source of supply.

This empowering human characteristic could be used to disempower Victims inside the misuse cycle. Becoming willing to observe that the narcissist's "standpoint" even while he or she's abusing you're something that the narcissist counts in order to maintain the cycle of abuse proceeding. An extremely empathic person is also a perfect viewer for the narcissist's shame ploys after violent episodes.

Narcissists believe that they could simply provide a sob story or even a faux Apology to eliminate the abuse, since they know that you will try to reevaluate their behavior and make excuses because of their own toxicity. They rely upon your capacity to forgive and plead with them after horrific episodes of mistreatment. By appealing to the compassion of the sufferers, malignant narcissists can escape liability for their actions, each and every moment. Empathic people often second-guess their conclusions to hold the narcissist liable since they might feel an extraordinary quantity of guilt when they view that the narcissist being penalized (whether by legislation or culture). So rather, they frequently feel compelled to safeguard their abusers instead of exposing them who they are.

3. Integrity.

Someone who keeps their sentence is incredibly appealing to a morally impoverished narcissist. People with ethics have an abundance of features that narcissists believe they could exploit to their own profit. After all, in case a sufferer feels it isn't in their ethical code to deceive or give up on a connection preemptively, who benefits? The narcissist that, on the other hand, doesn't have such ethical qualms.

While malignant narcissists feel little to no guilt for damaging their victims, their sufferers feel morally worried about retaliating, betraying the connection at all or stepping back out of their perceived duties to the narcissist. Their ethics, which may benefit them in relationships with additional curricular, like-minded people, become ammunition in a relationship with a narcissist -- a weapon used against them to destroy their sense of self and confidence on earth.

4. Resilience.

The capacity to "bounce back" from violent events is something that (counter intuitively sufficient) reinforces a sufferer's bond with a narcissist. Resilient people, such as youth abuse survivors, make for an outstanding source for your narcissist as they're in a position to withstand a huge quantity of pain without consuming. This is a gorgeous quality to have when it comes to tackling life's hardship, but at an unhealthy misuse cycle, a person's resilience becomes used against him or her to maintain them ensnared inside the narcissist's web of deceit.

In the end, exceptionally resilient People Are unlikely to give Up even after episodes of misuse despite the fact that they might have an improved capacity to detect risks in their surroundings. They'll choose to ignore their instincts and be eager to struggle for the connection against all likelihood, embracing a "savior" or "fighter" mindset as they work to maintain an ultimately unsustainable relationship. They might even quantify their love from the quantity of cruelty they set up with. This is also because of the nature of the injury bond they develop using a poisonous, abusive individual.

5. A high amount of sentimentality.

A sufferer Who's sentimental and enjoys deeply appeals to a Narcissistic person because they is able to utilize love-bombing (excessive flattery and compliments utilized to groom a sufferer) to allure to that individual's wants and desires easily. Since narcissists idealize their sufferers at the first phases of the connection, they can secure their faith with appealing to their craving for love. They like creating pleasurable memories they understand their victims will romanticize through the abusive phases of their connection.

Narcissists love toying with these victims' feelings; they understand they could mirror their sufferers intensely until they start to withdraw, so as to make that manufactured "soulmate" impact that will leave their aims depleted and hooked to them. Sentimental, empathic people are ideal fodder for narcissists to perform their reproductive pick-up artistry on -- they all need to do is control their goal's desire to locate a meaningful connection. That is an otherwise organic, human appetite that's sadly obscured by predatory forms.

"As discussion with you profits, the psychopath attentively assesses your character. Your character provides the psychopath an image of those traits and attributes you value in yourself. Your character can also show, to a astute observer, insecurities or flaws you would like to minimize or conceal from view. For a passionate student of human behavior, the psychopath will then softly test the internal strengths and needs which are a part of your personal self...The character of this psychopath -- that the "character" that the individual is communicating together -- doesn't actually exist. It was built on lies, carefully stitched together to entrap you. It's a mask, among the many, custom-made by the psychopath to match your specific psychological requirements and preferences" Dr. Paul Babiak and Dr. Robert Hare, Snakes In Suits: When Psychopaths Go To Work

The fantastic news? All these qualities and strengths also can Be utilized to detach yourself by the narcissist. It is possible to use your high amount of compassion to practice empathy on your own and realize that you're a divine-human being who doesn't deserve to be mistreated. It is possible to use your conscientiousness, integrity, and belief in humankind's good to join with other people who can encourage you and share your values. You can use it to pursue the love you really deserve -- with a man who really has a conscience. Most of all, you can make use of your own resilience to be a survivor and thriver after real life abuse. It is possible to use your power to break the bike, once and for all.

Chapter 4 Coping with a Narcissistic Personality

We tend to use the phrase narcissist to describe an individual who is egotistical and short on compassion. Nonetheless, it's essential to keep in mind that narcissistic personality disorder (NPD) is a valid mental health condition that a mental health practitioner needs identification.

However, people can display some narcissistic characteristics with no NPD. These may include:

- With an inflated sense of self
- needing constant praise
- taking Benefit of others
- Not Recognizing or caring about the needs of the others

To make matters more complex, individuals with NPD or Narcissistic tendencies are often quite sensitive to criticism, even despite their elevated self-esteem.

Here's a look at some sensible ways to manage someone With NPD or narcissistic trends -- and some strategies for recognizing when it is time to proceed.

1. Watch them for who they're

If they need to, those with real personalities are pretty good at turning on the charm. You may end up attracted to their expansive thoughts and promises. Additionally, this can make them incredibly well known in settings.

But before you get drawn in, see how they treat individuals when they are notion point." Should you grab them lying, manipulating, or intentionally disrespecting others, there is no reason to think they won't do precisely the exact same for you.

Regardless of what somebody with a genuine personality may Say, your needs and wants are probably unimportant to them. And if you attempt to bring up this matter, you might be met with resistance.

The very first step in dealing with somebody who has a narcissistic Character is only accepting that this is who they're -- there is not much you can do to change this.

2. Break the charm and stop focusing on them

Whenever there's a narcissistic character on your orbit, Ccareappears to reevaluate their manner. That is by design -- if it is positive or negative focus, those with real characters work hard to maintain themselves in the spotlight.

You may soon End up buying into this particular tactic, pushing aside your own needs to keep them satisfied.

If you are waiting to get a rest in their attention-seeking behavior, it might never come. However much you fix your life to match your own requirements, it is not likely sufficient.

If you must deal with a real-life character, do not enable them to infiltrate your awareness of self or establish your own world.

Take control and split out some "me time" Take care of yourself and keep in mind that it is not your job to correct them.

3. Speak up for yourself

There are times when blowing off something or walking away is a suitable answer -- choose your battles, right?

However, a lot depends upon the relationship. By Way of Example, dealing Using a supervisor, parent, or partner may involve different approaches than coping with a co-worker, sibling, or child.

Some individuals with narcissistic personalities like making other people squirm. If that is true, do your best not to get visibly flustered or reveal aggravation, as that is only going to advise them to last.

If it's somebody you want to stay close on your lifetime, then you owe it to yourself to talk. Try to get this done in a calm, gentle way.

You have to inform them their words and behavior affect your life. Be consistent and specific about what is not okay and how you anticipate being medicated. But prepare yourself to the very fact that they may just not understand -- or care.

4. Establish clear boundaries

Someone with a real life personality can be quite self-absorbed.

They May think they're eligible to go wherever they need; Suffering through your own things, or let you know how you ought to feel. Perhaps they give you unsolicited ideas and take credit for things you have done. Or compel you to discuss personal things in a general atmosphere.

They may also have small awareness of personal space Therefore, they Often cross a great deal of boundaries. More frequently than not, they do not even see them. That is why you've got to be abundantly clear about borders which are important for you.

Why would the effects matter? Because someone Using a narcissistic character normally starts to listen when things begin affecting them.

Just be certain it is not an idle threat. Talk about Consequences only if you are prepared to carry them out as mentioned. Otherwise they won't consider you another time.

FOR EXAMPLE

Say you have a co-worker who enjoys parking their large truck in a means which makes it almost impossible for you to back out. Start by firmly requesting them to be certain they leave you sufficient distance. Then, say the consequences of not respecting your wishes.

For Instance, If you cannot safely straight out, You'll Have their car towed. The crucial thing is to follow through and call the towing company that the next time it occurs.

5. Expect them to drive back

Should you stand up to somebody with a real life personality, It is possible to expect them to react.

As Soon as You speak up and place bounds, they may Return With a few requirements of their own. They might also attempt to manipulate you into feeling guilty or thinking that you are the one being foolish and commanding. They may make a play for sympathy.

Be ready to stand your own ground. Should you take a measure they will not take you seriously next time?

6. Bear in mind that you're not at fault

Someone with narcissistic personality disorder is not likely To acknowledge a mistake or accept responsibility for damaging you. Rather, they tend to try their own negative behaviors onto you or somebody else.

You May Be tempted to maintain the peace by accepting attributes; however, you don't need to belittle to salvage themselves.

You understand the reality. Do not let anybody take that away from you.

7. Locate a service system

Suppose you cannot prevent the Individual, attempt to build your healthful Connections and support community of individuals. Spending too much time at a relationship with somebody that has a narcissistic personality can leave you emotionally drained.

Rekindle old friendships and attempt to cultivate new ones. Get Together with household more frequently. In case your social circle is smaller than you would like, consider taking a course to research a new pastime. Get active in your neighborhood or volunteer for a charity. Does something which lets you meet more folks you feel comfortable with?

What's a HEALTHY RELATIONSHIP?

Spending a Great Deal of time with somebody who has a narcissistic Character can make it difficult to recall what a healthy connection actually feels like.

Here are a couple of hints to Search for:

• Equally People today listen and attempt to comprehend each other

• Equally Folks admit their mistakes and accept responsibility for them

• Equally People today feel as though they can unwind and be their authentic selves in the front of another

8. Insist on immediate actions, not promises

People with narcissistic characters are great at creating promises. They promise to do everything you need and to not do this thing you despise. They promise to normally do better.

As soon as they get what they need, the inspiration is gone. You Can't rely on their actions fitting their words.

Request what you need and stand your ground. Insist that You will only meet their orders once they have fulfilled yours.

Do not give in on this point. Consistency can help drive it home.

9. Understand a real person may want Professional assistance

Individuals with NPD often don't see an issue -- not with themselves. Because of this, it is unlikely they will ever look for expert counseling.

However, people with NPD often have other ailments, such as Substance abuse, or other mental health or character disorders. Possessing another ailment may be exactly what motivates someone to seek out assistance.

You can indicate that they reach out for professional Assistance, However, you cannot make them take action. It is absolutely their duty, none.

And Keep in Mind, while NPD is a mental health condition, it does not excuse poor or violent behavior.

10. Recognize when you need assistance

Regularly dealing with Somebody Who Has a narcissistic Character can take a toll on your mental and physical wellness.

For Those Who Have symptoms of stress, depression, or Physical anxiety disorders, visit your primary care physician. When you've got a checkup, you can ask for referrals to additional providers, like therapists and support teams.

Contact your family members and friends and telephone your service system into service. There is no need to go it alone.

When to Proceed

A few people with a narcissistic personality also can be verbally or mentally abusive.

Here are some indications of an abusive relationship:
- Name-calling, insults
- Patronizing, public humiliation
- Yelling, Threatening
- Jealousy, accusations

Other warning signals to watch for at another individual include:
- blaming you for all that goes wrong
- tracking your moves or trying to isolate you
- Notification You how you truly feel or should sense
- Routinely projecting their shortcomings
- denying Things which are obvious for you or trying to gaslight you
- trivializing your remarks and demands

But at what stage is it time to throw in the towel? Each connection has its ups and downs, right?

While this is accurate, it is generally better to leave the relationship if:
- You are emotionally abused
- You feel manipulated and controlled
- You have been mistreated or feel threatened
- You feel isolated
- that the Individual with NPD or a narcissistic character reveals signs of emotional illness or substance abuse, but will not get aid
- Your Physical or mental health was influenced

The Way to Handle Narcissistic Abuse

We are all capable of misuse once we're hurt or frustrated. We Might be guilty of criticizing, judging, withholding, and controlling, but a few abusers, such as narcissists, take insult to another level. Narcissistic abuse may be physical, psychological, psychological, physical, financial, or religious. Some kinds of psychological abuse aren't easy to identify, such as manipulation. It may consist of psychological blackmail, together with threats and intimidation to exercise control. Narcissists are masters of verbal manipulation and abuse. They could go so far as to make you doubt your personal senses, known as gaslighting.

The Motivation for Narcissistic Abuse

Remember that narcissistic personality disorder (NPD) and abuse exist on a continuum, which range from violence. Rarely will a narcissist take responsibility for her or his behavior. Normally, they refuse their activities and also fortify the misuse by attributing the victim. Malignant narcissists particularly are not bothered by guilt. They take delight in causing pain and are sometimes sadistic. They may be unscrupulous and so aggressive that they take part in anti-social behavior. Do not confuse narcissism with anti-inflammatory character disorder.

The aim of narcissistic misuse is electricity. These abusers Act with the aim to reduce or even harm other men and women. The most crucial point to consider about intentional abuse is the fact that it is intended to control you. Abusers' goals would be to maximize their control and ability, while generating uncertainty, uncertainty, and dependence in their sufferers. They would like to feel superior to prevent hidden feelings of inferiority. Knowing this can enable you. Like most offenders, regardless of their defenses of anger, arrogance, and self-inflation, they have problems with pity. Feeling humiliated and weak is the greatest fear. Knowing this, it is crucial to not take the words and actions of an abuser. This allows you to confront real life abuse.

Mistakes in Managing Abuse

When you overlook an abuser's motives, then you will naturally respond in a few of these unsuccessful ways:

- Appeasement -- Should you placate to prevent anger and conflict; it enables the abuser that sees it as weakness and a chance to apply more control.
- Pleading -- This also shows vulnerability, which narcissists hate in others and themselves. They may respond contemptuously with disgust or contempt.
- Withdrawal -- This can be a fantastic temporary strategy to collect your ideas and feelings but isn't a great strategy to take care of abuse.
- Arguing and Struggling -- Arguing above the truth compromises your energy. Most tormentors don't care about the truth, but just in justifying their place and being correct. Verbal arguments can easily rise to conflicts that drain and damage you. Nothing is obtained. You lose and may wind up feeling victimized, hurt, and despairing.
- Explaining and Defending -- anything beyond a straightforward denial of a false accusation leaves one open to more misuse. When you deal with content of what's being said and clarify and defend your position,

you endorse a person's appropriate to judge, approve, or mistreat you. Your response sends this message: "You have authority over my self-esteem. You've got the right to approve or disapprove of me. You are eligible to be my estimate."

• Searching Recognizing -- This will drive your behavior in the event you desperately wish to understand. It is predicated on the false expectation that a narcissist is interested in understanding you, while actually they're simply interested in winning a battle and with the superior position. Depending on the amount of narcissism, sharing your own emotions can also introduce you to hurt or manipulation. It is far better to talk about your feelings with somebody secure who cares about these.

• Criticizing And Complaining -- Even though they may act hard, abusers are essentially insecure, and within they are delicate. They can dish it, but cannot take it. Criticizing or complaining a bully can cause anger and vindictiveness.

• Hazards -- Making threats may result in retaliation or backfire if you do not carry them out. Never make a threat you are not prepared to enforce. Boundaries with immediate consequences are more successful.

- Denial -- Do not fall in the trap of jealousy by excusing, diminishing, or rationalizing abuse. And do not fantasize it is going to go away or improve some future moment. The more it goes on, the longer it develops, and the poorer you are able to become.
- Self-Blame -- Do not blame yourself for a person's activities and strive harder to be ideal. That is a delusion. You can not induce anybody to abuse you. You are solely responsible for your behavior. You won't ever be perfect enough to get a person to stop their behavior, which stems out of their insecurities maybe not you.

1. Confront abuse efficiently.

Letting abuse hurts your self-esteem. Thus, it's important to face it. That does not mean to fight and argue. It means standing your ground, talking for yourself calmly and clearly, and having bounds to shield your mind, feelings, and body.

2. Know your rights.

You Have to feel entitled to be treated with respect and that You've got specific rights, like the right for your own feelings, the right to not have physical intercourse if you fall, a right to privacy, a right to not be yelled at, touched, or even disrespected. If you have been mistreated a very long time (or as a kid), your self-esteem probably has been diminished. You might no longer expect yourself or possess confidence. Hunt treatment, obtain support, and see 10 Steps to Self-Esteem-The Ultimate Guide to Discontinue Self-Criticism and observe the webinar "How to increase your Self-Esteem."

3. Be assertive.

It requires practice and learning to prevent being aggressive or passive. Get How to Speak Your Mind--Be Assertive and Establish Limits as well as the webinar "How To Be Assertive." Try out these short term answers to coping with verbal putdowns:

4. be strategic.

Know what you need, especially what the narcissist needs, what your limitations are, and how you've got power in the connection. You are dealing with somebody exceptionally defensive with a character disorder. There are particular approaches to affecting. Read the scripts and steps in Addressing a Narcissist: 8 Steps to Boost Self-Esteem and Establish Boundaries with Difficult People.

5. Set boundaries.

Boundaries are principles that govern How You want to be handled. People will treat you the way you let them.

You have to understand what your boundaries are before you're able to communicate them. This usually means getting in touch with your feelings, listening to a body, understanding your rights, and studying assertiveness. They need to be explicit. Do not sign or expect people to read your thoughts.

6. Have consequences.
Once setting bounds, if they are ignored, it is important to convey and invoke consequences. These aren't risks, but actions that you take to safeguard yourself or fulfill your wants.

7. be educative.
Research also shows that narcissists have neurological deficits that influence their social reactions. Your Very Best approach is to instruct a Narcissist just like a kid. Describe the impact of their behavior, and supply Incentives and encouragement to get different behavior. This may involve communicating consequences. It requires preparation what you are likely to state without being psychological.

Chapter 5 The Way to Cure from narcissistic abuse

Core Insights from a Narcissistic Abuse Recovery Coach

As a narcissistic abuse recovery trainer, I provide several Basic insights to customers that anybody working to recuperate from real long-term abuse has to know.

1. A bigger Routine is in work. In case you've got a history of narcissistic connections, possibly with intimate partners or buddies or both, it can be that you've come out of a dysfunctional family dominated by adoptive parents or parents along with different kinds of psychological illness and/or dependence. Most of us experience narcissists in our lives, but those people who stick around for misuse have generally been conditioned to these relationships in youth. Connecting the past with the current is critical to knowing yourself, altering routines, and working on retrieval.

2. Denial is your own frenemy. Denial is your kid's first and only defense. After we are helpless and helpless it's preferable to deny deficiencies within our parents/caregivers compared to admit them to ourselves. It's also safer to blame ourselves for an issue

compared to question the standing of these people we rely on for our survival. The kid's urge to deny that the abuse and blame himself or herself for causing difficulties are details of human psychology, not aware decisions. But even though jealousy helps us endure as kids, it will become self-destructive in maturity. Provided that we're in denial we replicate unhealthy routines and don't safeguard ourselves and those we love from additional misuse. Breaking denial about a parent, partner, or other significant relationship is the first and often most difficult step in the restoration procedure.

3. Here is the main point about narcissism. For those people with psychological compassion for others' feelings and views, the narcissist's lack of compassion is incomprehensible. Emotional connectedness and compassion are youth developmental milestones the narcissistic personality misses. No matter how competent the narcissist could be in different locations, those developmental shortages are deep impairments. It is not an issue of locating the ideal means to describe your perspective, obtaining the narcissist to trust you, or ultimately proving your value. Narcissists do not care about your explanations, so you cannot win their faith,

along with your "value" ebbs and flows with the degree of status or service they believe you provide them. The pathological narcissist doesn't and never will care about your feelings or desires unless they chance to align somehow with what he or she desires. If you're the narcissist's spouse or child, this includes you.

4. There's No way around despair. Processing the fact of a connection having a narcissistic parent or spouse involves loss and despair. As an adult child, you grieve the loss of this loving parent you never needed, the healthful family and youth you overlooked, and, most basically, the Individual that you could happen to be with more assistance. As a spouse, you grieve the person that you fell in love together and believed you understood, the love that you did not get, and also the time you spent searching for something that never arrived --the confidence and intimacy that couldn't be. Mourning those declines is profoundly painful, and requires some time. Frequently we do anything to prevent the pain, deflecting and flushing ourselves with compulsions and addictions. A lot people spend years running out of despair just to find it staring us in the face within our 40s, 50s, or 60s, or perhaps afterward. Sitting with our despair,

acknowledging it moving through its entire array of emotion is essential for healing.

5. You've got Been through complicated injury. Long-term narcissistic abuse, especially of a young child, is a deep kind of injury. Kids in a real house encounter repeated, continuing assaults for their own sense of identity and wholeness that leave lasting physical and emotional consequences. Such kids or spouses frequently attest complicated injury, such as hypervigilance, depression, anxiety, and chronic pain and sickness. Knowing the consequences of complex injury and treating the indicators are crucial steps on the recovery path.

6. You can cure. Together with our capacity for suffering is a commensurate capability to cure. Healing occurs when we realize the larger patterns at work within our own lives, overcome denial, comprehend the fact of narcissism, and continue through our grief and injury on the street toward a much healthier and more joyful state of becoming.

How Can I Heal From Narcissistic Abuse?

What Exactly Does Narcissistic Abuse Do For You?

Narcissists utilize a Wide Selection of abusive approaches to Heal and hurt their victims. You may have found yourself in the receiving end of gaslighting, idealization and devaluation, sabotaging, stonewalling, deflection, and lots of different kinds of control and coercion.

All these kinds of narcissistic abuse may have a Devastating impact on your emotional and mental wellbeing, particularly if they're exercised during an extended period. Obviously, the specific consequences will change from 1 individual into another, but they might discuss some philosophical patterns you could have the ability to recognize on your own.

The Impacts of Narcissistic Abuse

Here is how narcissistic abuse may harm your psychological wellbeing:

• Reduced Self-esteem: among the most frequent consequences of narcissistic abuse is that a considerably impaired confidence. Even when you were assertive, self indulgent, and conscious of your values, you might now feel unlovable, unworthy, and feeble.

- Impaired Communication abilities: a connection with a narcissistic can also impact your communication style. You might find it really hard to express yourself openly and discuss your ideas and feelings. This can influence your friendships, career, and family life.
- Continuous Feelings of worthlessness and attribute: do you always internalize everybody else's issues and sense blame though you had nothing to do with them? This might also be a result of real life abuse.
- Insecure Attachment: narcissistic abuse can influence your potential connections, impairing and destabilizing your capacity to form healthy attachments on your own life. You can no longer feel secure opening up, or you could create a fear of jealousy.
- Narcissistic Tendencies: regrettably, narcissistic abuse may breed more narcissistic traits, particularly if it'sa parent or caregiver imposes it. You may start to exhibit narcissistic tendencies also, though you might not know about it.
- Superficial Behaviour: in order to shield yourself out of a narcissist while being in a relationship together, you want to be a tiny bit shallow. You've got to pretend happiness and gratification so as to prevent abuse rather than being honest and open.

What Happens After You Stand Up To Your Narcissist?

Although you might feel as standing up into a narcissist and Asking them for all of the heinous things they have done is a fantastic idea, you'll probably subject to more harm if you decide to do so. Here is the way the narcissist may respond if you face them:

- They may cater to your self, charming you to forgiving them
- They may Use different intimidation tactics to quiet you
- They may make fun of you and attack your weakest stains
- They may pretend to be dumb and cause you to question your sanity
- They may seriously about you to other folks, preventing you from friends and family

How Can You Feel After Having A Narcissist?

Teaming up with a narcissist is a large step. It may feel that a Lot like beating an addiction -- initially, it might be exceedingly painful, annoying, and disorderly, but it is going to give you a life back at the end. As soon as you part ways with your abuser, you ought to keep reminding yourself that there's a light at the end of the tunnel which you deserve to have happy relationships.

When the first stages are finished with, you'll feel liberated and at peace with yourself. You may learn how to trust your instinct, set healthy boundaries, and also be confident when dealing with different men and women. You may no longer need to walk on eggshells and browse the volatile psychological world of the narcissist. Finally, you may feel as though your healthy, powerful, and adorable self once more.

How Do You Recover From Narcissistic Abuse?

Recovering from real abuse can be a lengthy and Challenging process, but however big the obstacles might be, the travel will certainly be well worth it. Here are some useful suggestions if you are struggling with the aftermath of narcissistic misuse:

• Do not deny the misuse: there is no point pretending the narcissist's behaviors did not hurt you. Attempt to comprehend how you're affected by the misuse and confront the despairing head on.

• Establish clear Limits: if your puppy is still attempting to contact you, then you'll have to reveal severe advantage. It's quite possible you will feel enticed to remain in touch, but many experts concur that it is ideal for cutting off all communication if you're going to heal.

- Educate yourself empathy: be gentle on your own, however hard it can be. The abuse you endured is far out of the fault. Try to bear in mind that your abuser harms you since they have their own problems they will need to work on and concentrate on your wellbeing.
- Have a Support community: while spending time alone can be quite useful to your mental health, protracted isolation is seldom a fantastic idea. Rather, talk to your family and friends about your struggles and clinic vulnerability.
- Speak to Professionals: your loved ones members and friends might have the ability to offer you some aid, but they might not have the knowledge required to provide you with the help that you want. A Skilled relationship trainer will offer you resources you will need to Ease change and recover.

Conclusion

Are you currently in a relationship with someone who believes they are much superior for you and to everybody around them? Or perhaps your parent conducted your own lifetime, hoping nothing less than excellence in you and being jealous of your accomplishments -- so much so they discovered a way to earn your triumphs about them. Maybe you're married to somebody who is "hard" -- they need all of your attention, have an inflated ego, and therefore are often critical of you since things are constantly "your fault" In case you've got a tough, egotistical, and unemotionally accessible loved ones and feel as if you've got less self-confidence, have less freedom, or have given up your loved ones, hobbies, friends, or a livelihood for this Individual, you might be coping with real life abuse. Many narcissists will not enter treatment -- after all they do not believe there's anything wrong with them. Thus, narcissistic abuse retrieval is often for the sake of their spouse, child, or loved one who's being mistreated.

If you are in a relationship with a narcissist, it is important to seek expert assistance and help rebuild your confidence and revive your self-esteem. Remember that you're far better than you think you're -- the NPD individual's constant badgering has broken down your self-confidence and made you feel unworthy, but you're not -- you're a victim of abuse. Find a mental health professional who's specially trained in trauma recovery to assist in curing from real-life abuse. If you cannot leave the connection, a therapist can help you learn how to communicate effectively and set bounds so the narcissist can't benefit from you.

CPSIA information can be obtained
at www.ICGtesting.com
Printed in the USA
BVHW090110230421
605635BV00001B/332